Inner-City Poverty

OTHER BOOKS OF RELATED INTEREST

OPPOSING VIEWPOINTS SERIES
America's Youth
Child Welfare
Education
The Family
Health Care
The Homeless
Illegal Immigration
Juvenile Crime
Poverty
Teenage Pregnancy
Welfare
Work

CURRENT CONTROVERSIES SERIES
Crime
Drug Abuse
Hunger
Illegal Immigration
Marriage and Divorce
Minorities
Teen Pregnancy and Parenting

AT ISSUE SERIES
Guns and Crime
Immigration Policy
Single-Parent Families
Welfare Reform

Inner-City Poverty

Tamara L. Roleff, *Book Editor*

Daniel Leone, *President*
Bonnie Szumski, *Publisher*
Scott Barbour, *Managing Editor*
Brenda Stalcup, *Series Editor*

Contemporary Issues
Companion

GREENHAVEN
PRESS®

GALE

San Diego • Detroit • New York • San Francisco • Cleveland
New Haven, Conn. • Waterville, Maine • London • Munich

LIBRARY OF CONGRESS CATALOGING-IN-PUBLICATION DATA

Inner-city poverty / Tamara L. Roleff, book editor.
    p. cm. — (Contemporary issues companion)
Includes bibliographical references and index.
ISBN 0-7377-0840-9 (pbk. : alk. paper) — ISBN 0-7377-0841-7 (hb. : alk. paper)
    1. Poverty—United States. 2. Urban poor—United States. 3. Public welfare—
United States. 4. Inner cities—United States. 5. United States—Economic
conditions—2001– . I. Roleff, Tamara L., 1959– . II. Series.
HC110.P6 I56 2003
362.5'0973'091732—dc21

2002023639

Printed in the United States of America

CONTENTS

Foreword 7

Introduction 9

Chapter 1: An Examination of Inner-City Poverty

1. The Black and White Face of Poverty 14
   Richard Harwood

2. The Welfare Queen Stereotype 17
   Risa E. Kaufman

3. Crime Rates in Poor Neighborhoods 20
   Rebecca M. Blank

4. The Struggles of Young Immigrants in Urban America 25
   Somini Sengupta

5. Low-Wage Earners: Trapped in Poverty 32
   Marcia Passos Duffy

6. The Myth of Widespread American Poverty 35
   Robert Rector

Chapter 2: The Causes of Inner-City Poverty

1. Various Theories on the Causes of Poverty 45
   Harrell R. Rodgers Jr.

2. The Economic Factors Behind Long-Term Poverty 57
   Rebecca M. Blank

3. The Lack of Job Opportunities in the Inner City 63
   Helene Slessarev

4. Single-Parent Families Are More Likely to Be Poor 68
   Patrick F. Fagan

5. Immigration Is Responsible for the Rising Poverty Rate 79
   Linda Thom

Chapter 3: Solving the Problem of Inner-City Poverty

1. A "Living Wage" Is Necessary to Help the Working Poor 86
   Neal Peirce

2. A "Living Wage" Will Not Eliminate Poverty 89
   Nathan Karp

3. Welfare Reform Is Helping the Poor Move Out of Poverty 92
   Aimee Howd

4. The Mixed Results of Welfare Reform 98
   Christina Duff

5. Workfare: Successes and Failures 101
   Heather MacDonald

6. Corporate Involvement in Job-Training Programs   112
   Christina Nifong
7. Government Support of Faith-Based Initiatives Can Help
   Reduce Poverty   115
   George W. Bush
8. The Government Should Not Rely on Religious Charities
   to Help the Poor   121
   Polly Morrice
✓9. A Practical Alternative to Public Housing Projects   124
   Howard Husock
10. Providing Better Housing for the Poor   128
   Alexander von Hoffman

Chapter 4: Life in the Inner City: Personal Accounts
1. Living in Fear   137
   Earl Shorris
2. The Responsibilities of an Inner-City Grandmother   142
   Betty Washington, as told to Elijah Anderson
3. Stretching the Welfare Check   148
   David Zucchino
✓4. Trying to Leave the Inner City   156
   Janie Bryant

Organizations to Contact   165

Bibliography   169

Index   172

FOREWORD

In the news, on the streets, and in neighborhoods, individuals are confronted with a variety of social problems. Such problems may affect people directly: A young woman may struggle with depression, suspect a friend of having bulimia, or watch a loved one battle cancer. And even the issues that do not directly affect her private life—such as religious cults, domestic violence, or legalized gambling—still impact the larger society in which she lives. Discovering and analyzing the complexities of issues that encompass communal and societal realms as well as the world of personal experience is a valuable educational goal in the modern world.

Effectively addressing social problems requires familiarity with a constantly changing stream of data. Becoming well informed about today's controversies is an intricate process that often involves reading myriad primary and secondary sources, analyzing political debates, weighing various experts' opinions—even listening to firsthand accounts of those directly affected by the issue. For students and general observers, this can be a daunting task because of the sheer volume of information available in books, periodicals, on the evening news, and on the Internet. Researching the consequences of legalized gambling, for example, might entail sifting through congressional testimony on gambling's societal effects, examining private studies on Indian gaming, perusing numerous websites devoted to Internet betting, and reading essays written by lottery winners as well as interviews with recovering compulsive gamblers. Obtaining valuable information can be time-consuming—since it often requires researchers to pore over numerous documents and commentaries before discovering a source relevant to their particular investigation.

Greenhaven's Contemporary Issues Companion series seeks to assist this process of research by providing readers with useful and pertinent information about today's complex issues. Each volume in this anthology series focuses on a topic of current interest, presenting informative and thought-provoking selections written from a wide variety of viewpoints. The readings selected by the editors include such diverse sources as personal accounts and case studies, pertinent factual and statistical articles, and relevant commentaries and overviews. This diversity of sources and views, found in every Contemporary Issues Companion, offers readers a broad perspective in one convenient volume.

In addition, each title in the Contemporary Issues Companion series is designed especially for young adults. The selections included in every volume are chosen for their accessibility and are expertly edited in consideration of both the reading and comprehension levels of the audience. The structure of the anthologies also enhances accessibility. An introductory essay places each issue in context and provides helpful facts such as historical background or current statistics and legislation that pertain to the topic. The chapters that follow organize the material and focus on specific aspects of the book's topic. Every essay is introduced by a brief summary of its main points and biographical information about the author. These summaries aid in comprehension and can also serve to direct readers to material of immediate interest and need. Finally, a comprehensive index allows readers to efficiently scan and locate content.

The Contemporary Issues Companion series is an ideal launching point for research on a particular topic. Each anthology in the series is composed of readings taken from an extensive gamut of resources, including periodicals, newspapers, books, government documents, the publications of private and public organizations, and Internet websites. In these volumes, readers will find factual support suitable for use in reports, debates, speeches, and research papers. The anthologies also facilitate further research, featuring a book and periodical bibliography and a list of organizations to contact for additional information.

A perfect resource for both students and the general reader, Greenhaven's Contemporary Issues Companion series is sure to be a valued source of current, readable information on social problems that interest young adults. It is the editors' hope that readers will find the Contemporary Issues Companion series useful as a starting point to formulate their own opinions about and answers to the complex issues of the present day.

INTRODUCTION

Cities, with their promise of plentiful work, have always been a magnet for poor people from rural areas and small communities. However, these migrants to the cities typically find that they are only eligible for low-paying, unskilled jobs. Furthermore, cities generally have a higher cost of living than rural areas, so these workers often have to cope with unexpected expenditures. The result is that large cities have a disproportionate share of low-income workers compared to the suburbs and rural areas. According to the U.S. Census Bureau's statistics for 2000, out of the 31 million impoverished people in the United States, nearly 13 million live in America's inner cities.

In addition, inner cities have a high proportion of residents who are African American, Hispanic, or members of other racial and ethnic minorities. This phenomenon can be explained in part by looking at the history of the mass migration of southern blacks to northern cities that began in the early years of the twentieth century. These newcomers to the North hoped to find better jobs and a respite from southern racism. When looking for housing, however, they met with massive resistance from whites who did not want blacks living in their neighborhoods. Refused entry to desirable white neighborhoods, blacks were forced to live in the cities' dilapidated and overcrowded slums.

During the 1950s and 1960s, in an attempt to improve this situation, many cities built large, subsidized public housing projects. The theory was that if poor urban families were given a healthy alternative to the slums, they would be able to get ahead financially and eventually attain the American dream of buying their own home. Despite the cities' good intentions, however, this plan backfired. Established communities of more affluent residents fought plans to have the projects constructed near them; this opposition, according to authors Dennis Roncek, Ralph Bell, and Jeffrey M.A. Francik, "led to massive, segregated housing projects, which become ghettos for minorities and the economically disadvantaged." Instead of providing a safe haven for the poor, the high-density projects isolated the residents from the rest of the city. Soon they became hotbeds for all kinds of societal ills, such as vandalism, gangs, drug dealing and its associated crimes, the breakdown of the family, and an increase in illegitimate births.

Three public housing projects became especially notorious as centers of crime and urban blight: the Cabrini-Green and Robert Taylor projects in Chicago and the Pruit-Igoe project in St. Louis, Missouri. The projects in Chicago consisted of 109 high- and low-rise apartment blocks that covered two square miles and housed approximately forty thousand people, while the Pruit-Igoe project housed about ten thousand people at its peak. Crime in these neighborhoods reached such high levels that the projects became unlivable. Pruit-Igoe was torn down in 1976, only twenty-two years after it was built. In 1995, the Department of Housing and Urban Development took over Cabrini-Green and Robert Taylor, instituting a redevelopment project that involved replacing many of the original structures with new, lower-density buildings.

There are several reasons why public housing projects turned into crime-infested ghettos. In high-density neighborhoods, residents have trouble identifying who is a neighbor and who is not, so they are less likely to watch out for one another. The residents also have little incentive or spare income to maintain their apartments. Vandalism and destruction become a permanent part of the landscape, discouraging any attempts to keep the area nice. In addition, the majority of poor migrants to the cities are teenagers and young adults, who, as study after study has shown, comprise the segment of the population most responsible for gang violence, drug abuse, and crime. All these factors come together to encourage criminals to use the projects as a home base.

Also contributing to the impoverishment of the inner cities is the recent change in the cities' economic base. Whereas American cities used to be the major hubs for typical blue-collar jobs in manufacturing and transportation, during the last few decades, they have increasingly shifted to more white- and pink-collar jobs in administration, technology, and product information and service. This transformation from providing goods to providing services has also changed the educational requirements needed for employment. Generally, the new businesses require higher levels of education than were necessary for the old blue-collar jobs. These changes have not boded well for the inner-city poor, who on average tend to lack a high school degree.

Certain types of low-skilled and unskilled jobs have increased nationwide during this same time period—but not in the inner city. For example, the fast-food industry is experiencing rapid growth and desperately needs people to fill nonadministrative positions. John Kasarda, in a paper on the redistribution of jobs and people in the United States, explains why the increase in fast-food jobs has not helped the inner-city poor:

> Unfortunately, essentially all of the national growth in entry-level and other low-education requisite jobs have accrued in the suburbs, exurbs, and non-metropolitan areas far removed from growing concentrations of poorly educated urban minorities.

The inner-city poor, who often must rely on public transportation, are therefore at an extreme disadvantage. Frequently they are unable to reach the sites of these new jobs, or they must commute for several hours each day. Furthermore, the fast-food industry and other low-skilled service jobs usually pay much less than the old blue-collar factory positions did. With little prospect of finding a job that pays well within commuting distance, many inner-city residents drop out of the labor force entirely and rely on other means of support, such as welfare. As inner-city children and teens see their families and neighbors increasingly giving up on finding work, they may begin to consider living on welfare an acceptable way of life.

Yet some poor people do manage to find jobs that pay a living wage and allow them to move their families out of the impoverished inner city to safer urban areas or even to the suburbs. However, this trend itself seems to contribute to the plight of the inner cities. During the 1940s, 1950s, and early 1960s, families of all different income levels—poor, working poor, and middle class—typically lived together in the same urban neighborhoods. As long as working- and middle-class families remained in a particular neighborhood, businesses and stores were there to serve them. But when middle-class families, followed by working-class families, began fleeing to the suburbs in the late 1960s, these neighborhoods soon came to be populated only by the most disadvantaged residents—who some social scientists label the "ghetto underclass."

William Julius Wilson, author of *The Truly Disadvantaged*, believes that the working class and middle class served as a "social buffer" that protected inner-city neighborhoods from the long-term effects of unemployment. He argues that

> even if the truly disadvantaged segments of an inner-city area experience a significant increase in long-term spells of joblessness, the basic institutions in that area (churches, schools, stores, recreational facilities, etc.) would remain viable if much of the base of their support comes from the more economically stable and secure families. Moreover, the very presence of these families during such periods provides mainstream role models that help keep alive the perception that education is meaningful, that steady employment is a viable alternative to welfare, and that family stability is the norm, not the exception.

When the "social buffer" consisting of the employed working and middle class is removed, Wilson contends, the residents of poor neighborhoods become socially isolated and are no longer able to participate in mainstream activities. For example, they lose their network of employed friends and family, significantly reducing their opportunities for finding a job. In addition, children have little chance of sustained contact with family members or neighbors who are gainfully employed. According to Wilson, few inner-city children learn the link between education and employment; they tend to be unmotivated students, as indicated by the fact that inner-city schools typically have dropout rates of 50 percent or more. Furthermore, he adds, the lack of available and attractive jobs and the absence of a stable, employed population to serve as role models increases the likelihood that inner-city residents will turn to crime or drugs. The result, he concludes, are inner-city neighborhoods that "are plagued by massive joblessness, flagrant and open lawlessness, and low-achieving schools" and "avoided by outsiders," which further contributes to the neighborhoods' isolation.

The reasons behind inner-city poverty are many and complex. Perhaps the most important step in easing, or even eradicating, the problem is increasing public awareness of the existence and extent of inner-city poverty. To this end, *Inner-City Poverty: Contemporary Issues Companion* offers an overview of various aspects of this pressing issue. The authors included in this volume explore the world of urban poverty, examine proposed solutions and their effectiveness, and provide several personal perspectives on living in the world of the inner city.

CHAPTER 1

AN EXAMINATION OF INNER-CITY POVERTY

Contemporary Issues
Companion

THE BLACK AND WHITE FACE OF POVERTY

Richard Harwood

In the following selection, former *Washington Post* columnist Richard Harwood maintains that the media promulgates the myth that most poor Americans are black. In reality, he states, far more whites than blacks receive welfare or other types of public assistance, and more white children grow up in poverty than black children do. Furthermore, Harwood points out, the media image of the poverty-stricken black mother disregards the reality that, in all income groups, a higher percentage of black women than white women are employed. He contends that society's focus on black poverty leads many people to ignore the greater problem of white poverty and perpetuates an unrealistic and unflattering perception of blacks.

Jesse Jackson a couple of years ago chastised the media for stereotyping black Americans as a race of losers and misfits. "A black mask," he said, "has been put on the face of poverty. We must whiten the face of poverty to change the dynamics of the debate."

More Whites Are Poor

That wouldn't be hard to do if the media were so inclined. It's no secret to anyone but the press that white poverty and welfare dependency in America exist on a far greater scale than poverty and dependency in any other racial group. The Census Bureau in 1994 counted 25.4 million poor whites and 10 million poor blacks, a social reality rarely reflected in newspapers, magazines or the broadcast media.

Nearly twice as many white as black children are growing up in poverty-stricken homes. Far more whites than blacks are on the welfare rolls, as Jackson noted. Far more whites than blacks are getting food stamps, housing subsidies, health care through Medicaid and other forms of public assistance. The fact that the incidence of poverty and dependency is much higher among blacks and Hispanics than among whites doesn't change in the slightest the dimension or the social implications of the problems faced by these 25 million white Americans. And it certainly doesn't justify the unbalanced news coverage of social and economic distress in the United States.

Jesse Jackson is not alone in decrying the overemphasis of the press on black poverty and dysfunction. A recent series in *The Washington Post* on the travails of a black welfare mother trying to turn her life around inspired a small firestorm of protest by black readers, the paper's ombudsman reported: "Many of the critics were African American women. They were furious at *The Post* for using—yet again, they stressed—an image that plays into the most virulently persistent narrow-minded notions: that the face of welfare is black and female. That young black women are lazy, baby-bearing drags on society."

Social and Economic Status

The anger of these readers is understandable. For years a higher percentage of black than of white women has been gainfully employed in the labor force. Nearly 60 percent are in non-clerical, white-collar jobs, hundreds of thousands of them in managerial and professional positions. The number of black professional women rose 125 percent in a single decade, 1982 to 1992; the number of black women in corporate managerial positions rose by 64 percent in roughly the same period. These ranks swell each year as black women graduate in growing numbers (more than 100,000 in 1996) from colleges, universities and professional schools. Already, black females with AB degrees or higher earn more on average than white females with the same credentials.

The rise of these women in social and economic status and in their ability to influence political and economic institutions is a story far less familiar to the American people—and to the world— than tales of failure and lives of misery. That is generally true of black America as a whole.

The Journal of Blacks in Higher Education recently published a statistic from the American Booksellers Association that I have never seen in the "prestige press." Every 90 days black Americans buy roughly 10 million books—about 40 million a year.

That would come as no surprise to retailers, manufacturers and marketing gurus, who are well aware of the significant buying power of black consumers: more than $300 billion a year. They have known for years that black middle-class families are far more likely than the average American family to belong to book clubs, to collect stamps, to travel by train, to play tennis and buy good wines. The marketing bible, *American Demographics*, reported in 1996 that the "millions of middle-class and upper-class black households" represent one of the most lucrative and quality-conscious consumer markets in the country. They have up-scale tastes and the money to satisfy them. They are less likely than whites to patronize discount stores such as Walmart or K-Mart and more likely to shop in specialty and department stores."

Black households on average are more loyal than white households to brand-name products; they aren't looking for cheap substitutes. The black household spends 40 percent more each year on average than the non-black household on personal care services for women, 24 percent more on personal care services for men, 17 percent more on baby clothes, more on jewelry, electronic products, medical supplies, women's accessories and so on.

And despite popular conceptions to the contrary, blacks are rapidly becoming suburbanites. More than 60 percent of the black population of metropolitan Washington lives in the suburbs. In Atlanta the figure is 64 percent, in Miami 74 percent, in Los Angeles 58 percent, in San Francisco 43 percent. The incomes of black married couples have reached virtual parity with white household incomes.

This is mundane stuff to the demographers, adding up to a sort of Huxtable portrait of the black middle class which the media tend to ignore in their preoccupation with the aberrant aspects of American life. Beyond that, journalists through most of the twentieth century have seen themselves as patrons of the poor and the maimed. The mission is to comfort the afflicted, and who among us has been more afflicted than black Americans?

The problem is that in going about that task with such zeal we leave in our wake stereotypes that have unintended but very painful effects. One of them, in this case, is that in the desire to do something about black poverty, we gloss over or ignore the very real and very big problem of white poverty. Another is that we create an unwarranted and unflattering perception of black Americans as a pitiable race. That perception is unhelpful and it is untrue.

THE WELFARE QUEEN STEREOTYPE

Risa E. Kaufman

According to Risa E. Kaufman, one of the most prevalent stereotypes concerning the poor is the image of the "welfare queen"—a
black, unemployed, unwed mother with many children. Kaufman
explains that welfare queens are characterized as able-bodied
women who are too lazy to work, who manipulate and exploit
the welfare system for their own gain (for example, by having
additional children out of wedlock in order to increase their benefits), and who pass on their irresponsible values to their children. Many elements of the welfare queen myth are untrue, she
notes; for instance, the average welfare recipient does not have
more children than the average mother who is not on welfare.
The author concludes that the welfare queen stereotype is racially
oppressive and is used to hold welfare recipients responsible for
their plight instead of addressing the causes of poverty. Kaufman
is a former staff attorney for the National Organization for
Women Legal Defense and Education Fund.

Historically, stereotypes and myths of the poor have informed the creation, shape and scope of public assistance programs. Specifically,
myths which differentiate the "undeserving" poor from the "deserving" poor justify punitive welfare policies on the basis that certain
populations (unwed mothers, "lazy" and shiftless paupers) are responsible for their poverty and must be discouraged and prevented from
depending upon public assistance. As the welfare population, particularly Aid to Families with Dependent Children (AFDC), became
increasingly black, the stereotypes associated with the "undeserving
poor" fused with stereotypes that have traditionally justified systemic
discrimination against African-Americans. In particular, despite the
fact that large numbers of white women also receive welfare, the popular conception of the "typical" AFDC recipient has become an
unmarried, unemployed black urban woman with many children.
According to children's rights advocate Marion Wright Edelman, this
has resulted in the use of "welfare" as a code word for race. Thus, the

Excerpted from "The Cultural Meaning of the 'Welfare Queen': Using State Consti-
tutions to Challenge Child Exclusion Provisions," by Risa E. Kaufman, *NYU Review
of Law and Social Change*, 1997. Copyright © 1997 by *NYU Review of Law and Social
Change*. Reprinted with permission.

stereotyped image of the "welfare queen" enables racist ideology to manifest itself in seemingly "neutral" welfare legislation.

This article explores the gendered, racist mythology that informs child exclusion provisions. [Child exclusion provisions penalize welfare recipients who have additional children by denying them otherwise automatic increases in benefits when children are born.] In the context of this mythology, it may be argued that child exclusion provisions are racially discriminatory due to their racist motivation, as well as the effect they have of perpetuating and reinforcing the stereotypical image of the "welfare mother."

Pervasive Images

One of the most pervasive images of the poor is that of the "underclass" or "counter-culture" poor, which links blacks with poverty through representations of "able bodied persons with virtually permanent dependence on cash welfare . . . especially seen as unmarried minority women bearing children with a succession of minority men who are, at best, on the fringes of criminal activity," according to Hugh Heclo in *Confronting Poverty*. Consequently, policy approaches to poverty are predicated on an assumption that poor, urban blacks suffer from "cultural inferiority," which is seemingly illustrated by the disintegration of the family and the absence of a strong work ethic, and characterized by out-of-wedlock births, chronic unemployment, welfare dependency, teen pregnancy, drug abuse, alcohol addiction, and criminal activity. This use of *cultural* inferiority to explain the poverty experienced by inner city blacks has replaced the use of *racial* inferiority to explain the subordinated status of blacks.

Gender is infused into these images of the "underclass" via the "welfare queen." "Content to sit around and collect welfare, shunning work and passing on her bad values to her offspring," Patricia Hill Collins notes in *Black Feminist Thought*, the welfare queen is portrayed as being lazy and irresponsible. Her personal faults cause her own poverty and that of her children. This myth of the welfare queen stems from other traditional stereotypes, or what Dorothy E. Roberts terms "controlling images," of black women, which devalue black motherhood and blame black mothers for the problems of the black family. One particular image at the root of this myth is that of Jezebel, the promiscuous slave woman, whose extreme sexuality and fertility rendered her an unfit mother.

An outgrowth of Jezebel, the welfare queen is invoked as a clear example of the "cultural inferiority" of poor urban blacks and is used to justify shifting the focus of welfare policy from addressing structural causes of poverty to blaming the victims themselves. Specifically, as Nina Perales writes, the "welfare queen" is "a woman of color who manipulates and exploits the welfare system, scorns lasting or legalized relationships with men, and has a series of children out of wedlock in order to continue her welfare eligibility." When the welfare queen is blamed for perpetuating the black underclass by producing too many economically unproductive children, welfare policies aimed at modifying her perceived behavior focus on limiting her fertility. Thus, welfare reform measures which seek to prevent her from having additional children are justified. Child exclusion provisions predicated on discouraging welfare recipients from having additional children while on welfare are intricately connected with the image of the welfare queen.

The Negative Impact of Stereotypes

The transmission of stereotyped images of welfare recipients and their use in informing legislation such as child exclusion provisions are counter-productive. In reality, although a disproportionate percentage of African-American women receive welfare, blacks and whites receive welfare in approximately equal numbers. Furthermore, the number of children born to an average welfare recipient is no larger than the number born to her non-recipient counterpart. Perhaps most importantly, social science research indicates that receiving welfare does not motivate recipients to get pregnant. As a welfare measure justified by false assumptions about welfare recipients, the child exclusion provision does not effectively address the issue of poverty.

In addition to being counter-productive, stereotyped images of welfare mothers are racially oppressive. These images provide justification for economic and racial subordination. One way in which this is achieved is through the function and creation of the "other." In characterizing whites as the "norm," and blacks as deviant from that norm, stereotypes based on racist ideology arrange blacks and whites in "oppositional categories in hierarchical order," in the words of Kimberle Williams Crenshaw, placing whites in a dominant position relative to the subordinate status of blacks. The social construction of blacks in opposition to whites was a necessary step in justifying and enabling slavery, which represents the ultimate fusion of economic and racial domination. This creation of the "other" is significant in the creation of welfare policy as well. It fuels the stereotypes of welfare recipients by driving the distinction between deserving and undeserving poor, in turn justifying inadequate expenditures on public assistance programs. It also enables shifting the focus of welfare policy from the structural and societal causes of poverty to the moral, "cultural" failings of the poor. Examining the stereotypes which have informed the welfare debate (and then have been transmitted by the resulting welfare policies) exposes the role of child exclusion provisions in perpetuating racial subordination.

CRIME RATES IN POOR NEIGHBORHOODS

Rebecca M. Blank

In the following excerpt from her book *It Takes a Nation: A New Agenda for Fighting Poverty*, Rebecca M. Blank writes that many Americans perceive the poor—especially those living in urban ghettos—as being likely to commit violent crimes. In a small number of inner-city neighborhoods, Blank admits, crime rates have soared in recent years, particularly homicides of young black men and the use of crack cocaine. However, she argues, it is important to realize that not all of the poor people who live in these high-crime neighborhoods are criminals or drug users. Instead, she explains, most are law-abiding citizens who struggle to protect their children and other loved ones from the violent acts committed by a small percentage of their neighborhood's population.

The "dangerous poor" is an image that has often haunted American discussions of poverty. Disproportionately, in an immigrant nation, the poor have always been the most recent immigrant group, which means they have always been "the other"—the strangers who dress differently, talk with strange accents, or follow strange customs. The stranger, the one who is different, has always caused fear. The best example of this, of course, has been African Americans, who are hardly the most recent immigrant group but who bear the scars of racism that defines them as "dangerous strangers" even after centuries of life in America.

Thus, one of the most frequent arguments for revitalizing urban ghettos or preventing child poverty is not to improve the well-being of the poor, but to increase the well-being of the rest of society. As the argument is often presented, poor children must be educated and given a sense of future opportunities to prevent them from turning to crime, to drugs, or to gangs, and thereby threatening the security of the nonpoor. Urban ghettos must be rehabilitated so that their blight does not spread to other neighborhoods.

The Truth About Crime

A discussion of crime and poverty is difficult because many Americans have come to believe "facts" about crime that are not true. Contrary to popular perception, reported victimization rates for most crimes have declined since the 1970s. Figure 1 shows the trends over time in the rate (per 1,000 persons age 12 and over) of reported crimes of violence against persons (rape, robbery, and assault), crimes of theft against persons, and household burglary. Since the mid-1970s, crime rates in these aggregate categories and in their subcategories have declined. The only category of crime whose rate has increased is motor vehicle theft. All other forms of crime were occurring at a lower rate in 1991 than they were in 1980. This is true even if the data are disaggregated by city, suburb, and rural area. Crime rates in America have decreased. For most Americans, life is safer now than it was fifteen years ago.

Despite these data, many of us live with a sense of threat. Public discussion of the need for more police and better law enforcement is constant. Polls indicate that over half of all people say that crime has increased in their neighborhood in the early 1990s. In 1993, according to Kathleen Maguire and Ann L. Pastore, 71 percent of respondents indicated that "halting the rising crime rate" was a serious problem on which we were spending too little money. Why are we so frightened? There are at least three reasons.

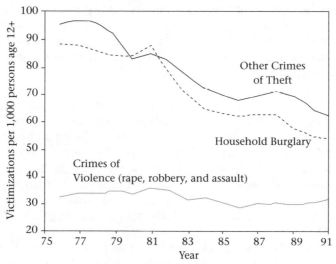

Figure 1. Victimization Rates for Crimes of Violence, Theft, and Household Burglary, 1975–1991

Kathleen Maguire et al., *Sourcebook of Criminal Justice Statistics, 1992*, Washington, DC: U.S. Government Printing Office, 1993.

Why Americans Are Frightened

First, our sense of safety is heavily shaped by media reporting of crimes.
The national news is dominated by reporting from a few major urban
areas, and by the most horrible crimes in those areas. Murder rates
rose in Chicago and New York from 1980 to 1993, and soared in
Washington, D.C., where the murder rate in 1993 was three times
larger than in New York City. But in many other cities (both big cities
such as Los Angeles or in smaller-sized cities), murder rates have fallen
or remained constant. As long as much of our national news comes
from New York and D.C., our sense of reality may be shaped by
impressions that do not apply to our own towns.

Local news shows have also increasingly focused on the most grue-
some stories. The motto for many local news shows has become, "If it
bleeds, it leads." This leaves viewers with an impression that local
crime is horrendous and prevalent, without giving them any sense of
the actual probability that such crimes will affect them.

*Second, many of us regularly watch movies or TV shows that feature mur-
der and threat as their primary plot device.* There is accumulating evidence that watching fictional portrayals of crime makes people feel
more threatened in their daily life. Regularly viewing stories about
conspiracies, stalkings, murders, kidnappings, and assault on a nightly
basis persuades too many people that these events are likely occur-
rences in their neighborhoods.

*Third, crime rates are rising among a few groups and in a few neighbor-
hoods, and these crime increases have received an enormous amount of
attention.* Among young men (particularly young black men) there
has been a shocking increase in murder, primarily through increased
gun violence. Rates of homicide among young black men between
ages 15 and 24 have almost doubled since 1985, and are *eight times*
the homicide rate among young white men of the same ages. In
urban ghetto neighborhoods, the incidence of handgun possession
and use has soared.

People of all ages in these communities live in fear of stray bullets,
often shot by teenagers who have little sense of the value of life. A
number of shocking incidents in major cities have received prominent attention. For instance, a seven-year-old living in the Cabrini
Green housing project in Chicago was shot in the head and killed as
he walked across the street to school; a five-year-old boy was killed
when several older boys dropped him out of a fourteen-story window
while his brother tried to fight them off. We listen to these stories
with horror and fear that *our* children may be at risk of equally inex-
plicable and random death.

Life expectancies for black men have fallen over the last ten years,
largely due to an increase in deaths from homicide. Homicides tend
to be densely concentrated in urban areas. For instance, a map of the
murders in Washington, D.C., shows several tight clusters of dots

around several easily identified streets and street corners, and only a slight scattering of dots elsewhere through the city. These deaths are not random, nor are all city dwellers at equal risk.

Drug Use

The picture for drugs is quite similar. Like crime, drug use has fallen over the past fifteen years. This is true of almost all types of illegal drugs, from cocaine to marijuana. On average, Americans are getting high less often. The most commonly used legal drug, alcohol, is also declining in use. Americans who drink are also more likely to drink lower-alcohol drinks (wine or beer) than in the past. Sales of hard liquor have waned.

Yet, like homicide, among some groups drug use is high. We have little data that tabulate drug use by income level, but the statistics indicate that illegal drug use is higher among younger people, men, those with less education, and those who are not working. While the data are admittedly limited, drug use within all of these demographic groups has declined since 1985, although these groups continue to have higher rates of drug use than other demographic groups. Interestingly, people in large metropolitan areas report lower rates of illegal drug use in the 1990s than people in smaller metropolitan areas.

One particular drug that has received a great deal of attention is crack cocaine. While overall cocaine use has declined, the spread of crack cocaine in certain city neighborhoods in the early and mid-1980s made available a drug that was relatively cheap and which produced an intense high. We have little formal data on crack use until the 1990s, when the national drug use surveys started to collect this information. By any measure, crack cocaine is used by a very small proportion of drug users. The share of persons reporting crack use is one-fifth of those who report overall cocaine use and one-twentieth of those who report marijuana use. Anecdotal evidence suggests that crack users are lower-income persons and concentrated in particular city neighborhoods.

Drugs and Women

Most troubling, the availability of crack cocaine appears to have led to increased use by women, who typically have had much lower drug usage and addiction rates. The phenomenon of "crack babies" has been a major problem for public hospitals in large urban areas, as babies born with crack addiction (and often with other health problems as well) demand special medical and nursing attention.

Just as the use of crack cocaine is limited to a small share of the population, however, the number of women with children who seriously use and abuse drugs remains relatively small. For instance, Doug Besharov of the American Enterprise Institute has estimated that no more than one or two percent of babies are born to women with crack addictions, approximately 30,000 to 50,000 births per year. Other more recent surveys have found numbers of the same magnitude or smaller. Even if we take the higher number and assume that all of these births were to poor women, this would constitute only about five percent of births to poor women. While I consider this number unacceptably high, it is obviously a problem within a small group of the poor population.

Drug use, gun violence, street crime, gang activities, and other forms of criminal behavior are all more prevalent in poorer areas, and highly prevalent in some of our poorest and most desperate urban neighborhoods. These are not problems to dismiss or to minimize. But there are two generalizations we must be careful not to make.

The Poor and Crime

First, not all poor persons who live in high-crime neighborhoods are part of a culture of crime and violence. In fact, criminal activity and serious drug abuse are, even in the poorest neighborhoods, the activity of a few. Their biggest victims are not those who live outside the neighborhood, but those who live within the neighborhood, trying to protect their children from the gangs, the guns, and the drugs. The primary reason to stop this activity is not because it threatens the middle classes who live 10 miles away, but because it threatens to destroy the lives of those who are trying to live resilient and healthy lives in poor communities. Low-income persons are three times more likely to be victims of violent crimes than are high-income persons. The fear of crime and victimization makes it much harder for mothers to protect their children, for schools to teach well, or for poor families to improve their lives.

Second, we should not ascribe to all poor persons the problems and behaviors of the few. Close to 90 percent of the poor live outside the urban ghetto neighborhoods that are most afflicted with drugs and crime. The visibility of violence and crime among a few groups of the poor should not be taken to indicate that most poor persons engage in this behavior. The steady declines in crime and drug rates among most demographic groups suggests that, if anything, fewer persons are engaged in these behaviors now than they were ten years ago.

While our information on the correlations between poverty, crime, and drug abuse is limited, the images that directly link poverty and crime are often badly overstated. Most people, at all income levels, do not participate in these activities. While concentrated problems of violence, particularly homicide, have increased in our poorest city neighborhoods, even here, the poor are more likely to be the victims than the perpetrators of such crimes. Serious problems of violence—often correlated with drugs—do exist, particularly among younger men in ghetto neighborhoods. These problems deserve serious attention. But the number of poor who participate extensively in these dangerous activities remains small.

THE STRUGGLES OF YOUNG IMMIGRANTS IN URBAN AMERICA

Somini Sengupta

In the following article, *New York Times* reporter Somini Sengupta describes a specific segment of the urban poor: teenaged immigrants who come to the United States on their own in search of a better life. Alone in a new country, these teenagers must support themselves, Sengupta writes; since most are here illegally, they usually end up taking exploitive jobs, working long hours for meager pay. The author explains that these young immigrants realize they need a good education in order to move up economically, but their jobs leave them with little time to attend school and do homework. They are also susceptible to the pressures of the inner city, such as joining gangs for protection. Sengupta compares today's young immigrants to those who arrived in the United States at the turn of the twentieth century, noting that it is much harder now for immigrant teenagers to achieve their educational and economic goals.

Monir was hardly among the huddled, hungry masses of Bangladesh when he arrived at Kennedy International Airport in 1996. His father was an engineer; everyone expected Monir would go to college and study accounting.

In Search of a New Life

What drove him from home was neither poverty nor war, just the sure specter of a dead-end future. Back in Dhaka, all but the wealthiest toiled through college only to hunt in vain for decent jobs. At 15, Monir took flight, in search of an American education, another life.

Now 18 and still struggling through his sophomore year of high school, Monir works late every night, packing takeout orders of Thai food. The fear of failure follows him like a ghost. It is there when he cannot get to school on time, when he realizes how far behind he is on his homework, when he spots a classmate who dropped out a while back, handing out fliers for an Indian restaurant in the East Village.

"I have those worries," Monir confessed quietly. "Maybe I'll end up like him."

They are elusive to official institutions, but youngsters like Monir are everywhere. They deliver pizza on rickety bicycles. They cut flower stems at the corner greengrocer. They peddle fake-label watches on the sidewalks of Manhattan and sprint at the sight of the police.

Over the last several years, a small but growing number of teen-agers—virtually all boys, some as young as 14 or 15—have arrived without their parents, much like the child immigrants of a century ago. Once here, they become New York's youngest immigrant workers, their cheap, nimble labor easily absorbed by the city's thriving service economy.

They come from countries where the poor go to work young. They know they are trading one hard life for another, but at least this one seems to come with some options. Here, on their own, they are free as birds, and yet they are trapped in an underground ruled in large measure by fear—of the immigration authorities, child welfare agencies, smugglers, thugs and bosses, past and potential. (That is why all of the youngsters interviewed for this article would give only their first names; some refused to be photographed.)

And immigration scholars and social workers wonder if they will ever be able to break free. Most are in this country illegally—and with rare exception, seem destined to remain so. Many come for education, and its promise of opportunity unimaginable in Dhaka, or whatever place they left behind. And yet, working long, hard hours to stay alive, they often find themselves too tired and tied down, and simply too poor, to get the education they need to move beyond the margins of the economy.

In short, they are like a lot of new immigrants. And yet they are not—because they are children, and they are alone.

Just how many there are cannot be known, but the few institutions that encounter them offer piecemeal evidence of their growing presence. The Immigration and Naturalization Service reports a fivefold increase in the number of unaccompanied minors entering the country illegally between 1995 and 1999. In fiscal year 1998, the agency had 4,284 such children in detention, the vast majority between 15 and 18. Officials say they expect many more to come from parts of Central America ravaged by Hurricane Mitch in 1998.

At the Chinatown Health Center, doctors report seeing many more children coming alone, especially from Fujian Province. English teachers at The Door, a SoHo youth center, say they have seen rising numbers of teen-agers coming alone from Mexico and Central America.

"It's really spiked, starting about three years ago," said Christopher Ambrose, the center's co-director. "It's just incredible to me that they're doing what they're doing all by themselves."

Among the ranks of teen-age immigrants to the city was a young man from Guinea named Amadou Diallo, whose American adventure began in 1996 at age 19 and ended in 1999 when, unarmed, he was killed by the police at the door to his apartment building in the Bronx. There are boys like Francisco, from Mexico, who run away defiantly, and those like Abdoulaye, from Senegal, who come with their parents' blessings. There are those like Monir who live on their own, perhaps with a roommate, and those who are taken in by relatives, like Jian, a Fujianese farmer's son, who shares a two-room tenement in Chinatown with an uncle and eight other men.

All are keenly, constantly aware of the gulf between them and the young people around them—many of them also poor, many also immigrants, but none quite so peculiarly alone. Jian is struck by this every time he runs into schoolmates from Qianyang, his village outside the city of Fuzhou. If they work, it is not to pay the rent. Their parents take care of that, and harangue them to finish their homework so they do not have to work in sweatshops all their lives.

Once, Jian invited his old best friend over to his apartment, and his friend gasped. "He said, 'I can't imagine you live here,'" Jian recalls. "We are like strangers."

A Life of Work

Francisco's day begins in the blue light before dawn, as the steel accordion gates of a lower Manhattan diner roll open for business. Francisco's territory is the grill, where he hovers over burgers and B.L.T.'s. To his left sits a vat of gurgling hot oil that has pocked his arms with a trail of burns. A Yankees cap shields his boyish, blessedly acne-free face.

Except Sundays, when he makes sandwiches at another deli, this is Francisco's world all week, from 4:30 A.M. till 3:30 in the afternoon. After work, there are lessons at The Door, where he has learned English and is now, after nearly a decade without a formal education, preparing for the high school equivalency exam. Then, home by 8 to his room in a basement apartment near Yankee Stadium, so he can shower, sleep and rise by 3 A.M. for another day at the grill.

He is 21 now, but Francisco's childhood died young, in the Oaxacan village of Etla. By the time he was 10, he was hopping trains to faraway towns, where he passed himself off as an orphan and ran errands in exchange for food, spare change, a set of new clothes.

His parents tried to wring the restlessness out of him, but without success. With the help of a friend already living in the Bronx, he found a smuggler, who for $900 led him across the border and onto a plane to New York. Francisco thinks he was 15 then.

Within weeks, he was sweeping the floors of a midtown garment factory, 10 or 12 hours every day, for $190 a week.

Finding work was always a breeze, though the terms of his employment were completely illegal. Under state law, school is mandatory for all those under 17. And youths between ages 16 and 18 are barred from working more than 28 hours a week when school is in session.

Once, cutting a swatch of linen, Francisco accidentally sliced off a piece of his left index finger. His boss dropped him in front of a hospital emergency room and left. When Francisco returned to work, the boss refused to take him back, saying he was too young.

"They really took advantage of me, huh?" Francisco said, chuckling. "I learned that after I left that job."

In Francisco's fiercely self-protective world, there is little time or inclination to play. Fear keeps him on the straight and narrow. Sometimes, he hangs out with a clutch of young Mexicans who live in his building, but he will not drink with them, for fear he will not make it to work on time. There are clubs he could go to, but he won't, for fear he will be swept up in a drunken brawl.

Perhaps what also keeps Francisco on his path of self-restraint is boys like Marcos. The two are strangers, but in a way, they are mirror images.

When Marcos left Oaxaca at age 12, he, too, was searching for money and education. Seven years later, he has not known a day of school, nor has he managed to learn English. He has been a dishwasher, a pizza deliverer and a prep cook. He has also been to Rikers Island and back.

Marcos has never really been out of trouble. At first, he was taunted in his East Harlem neighborhood as a "mojado," a wetback. Thugs repeatedly jumped him, taking what little money he made.

Soon, though, another band of thugs came to his rescue. They called themselves Los Vagos, the vagabonds, and they became his family. They tattooed a tricolor Virgin on his left arm; they made sure he was never attacked again.

But trouble continued to trail him. Within months, a knife fight at a soccer match got him six months in jail. And in December 1998, one of Los Vagos was shot and killed at a club on 116th Street; Marcos said he and seven other gang members were charged. He is out on bail, awaiting trial.

"We say this is the lost generation," said Brother Joel Magallan, a Jesuit who works for the Roman Catholic Archdiocese of New York as its liaison to Mexican immigrants. "I know a lot of parents who are trying to keep them in Mexico. They don't want their kids coming here."

Francisco may have run away at 15, but he never intended to stay away so long, he said. His goal was to earn enough money to establish a family business. In 1998, he wired home $11,000 in savings so his father could set up a garment factory. He had read that clothing was one of Mexico's chief exports. Nowhere had he read about the hurdles.

"You have to have big capital," he says now. "You have to have connections."

The lessons came too late. The five sewing machines bought with his savings now collect dust in Etla.

Changing Opportunity

The stories of Francisco and the others are a distant echo of the flood of teen-age immigrants a century ago. Back then, at the crest of the last great wave of immigration, Italian boys landed by themselves at Ellis Island and went to work hawking newspapers or hauling produce. Girls from Russia came alone to work in garment factories.

But if their ages and aspirations are in many ways the same, today's teen-age immigrants are landing on drastically changed shores.

Nancy Foner, an anthropologist who studies the city's immigration history, offered her own family's example. In 1905 or so, when he was 8 or 9, her grandfather came alone from Russia and joined a brother in Hartford. The sum of his American education was some time in night school as a working teen-ager, but by the time he retired, he was running a lucrative construction business in Queens.

Certainly, few immigrants of that era bounded up the economic ladder in one generation. Still, those with little schooling could find a factory job—often, a dirty job for low pay, but a job for life. Some could move from unskilled factory jobs to semi-skilled labor at slightly better pay. Some could even open small shops or factories. And since, with few exceptions, even those without formal papers did not face the constant threat of deportation, even the immigrant who did not succeed economically could establish a firm, legal foothold for the next generation.

"It's much harder to get ahead today, with as little education as my grandfather had," Ms. Foner explained.

Today's teen-age immigrants, by contrast, are unlikely to be legal and have few ways to change that. Unlike adults with marketable skills, they are unlikely to be sponsored by an employer, and few have resident family members to help them obtain a green card. And their immigration status, compounded by poverty, makes it extremely difficult to get the higher education that is ever more crucial to economic success. For illegal immigrants, a secure job of any kind has become harder to find.

So, while some will find a way to get ahead, most seem likely to drift from way station to way station in New York's economic underground, hoping, at best, to save enough money to set up a decent life back home.

"My guess would be that if you do not have fluency in English, if you do not have skills, if you do not have legal papers, you're going to work in a marginal, shadow economy," said David Reimers, a historian at New York University. "I don't see these people, in their lifetime, improving that much."

Whether most will end up staying or returning home is anyone's guess. For now, out there on the margins, they tend to fall below the radar of government agencies that deal with children. Given the choices here and at home, some academics and advocates say, it is probably just as well.

"It's a pretty sad thing to say that perhaps the best outcome would be let them work, leave them alone," said Hector Cordero-Guzman, a sociologist at the New School for Social Research. "Increased enforcement might not mean better life chances for these kids."

The Education Barrier

If college is the dream, Jian would seem closer than most. Even so, he feels it slipping away.

The first in his family to learn his letters, he is 20 credits shy of a high school diploma. Eight hours a day, he is in class at Manhattan Comprehensive Night and Day School, a school for older teen-agers. Four years after leaving China at age 17, his time is running out. He can attend public school free only until the end of his 21st year; he has just turned 21.

Weekends are spent behind the plexiglas of a Chinese takeout restaurant in New Jersey: 12-hour shifts both days, $70 a day. At first, his priorities puzzled his roommates. "They said: 'Why you want to study? You're not born here,'" he recalled.

Many young immigrants like him rarely venture outside Chinatown or learn English, he says. The prospect terrifies him. "You don't know English, you know how difficult life is," Jian said. "How about the future?"

For now, Jian pays $50 a month for a bed in a sixth-floor walk-up. The apartment is so cramped that he does morning sit-ups in bed, so noisy that he can start studying at the kitchen table only after everyone goes to sleep.

Jian considers himself an optimist and says he has no regrets about coming here. And recently, he was granted a rare boon—political asylum on the grounds of religious persecution. He is a Christian, with the dangerous habit of preaching to his classmates back home. He can become an American citizen in a few years.

Still, even with the security of asylum, even with a diploma, he says he will have to postpone college until he can climb his mountain of debt: the $40,000 that his parents borrowed from family and from the bank to have him smuggled to America. So after high school, Jian plans to get a full-time restaurant job and start repaying the loans. He does not know anyone who has gone to college here. He says it probably costs too much. "I'm not sure," he concluded, "but I think it's a lot of money."

Longing for Home

By the time Abdoulaye felt that adolescent urge to take flight from Senegal, nearly every house on his block in Kaolack had sent a young man abroad—to France, Italy and, in recent years, to the United States. At 19, made restless by a long strike at his university, Abdoulaye joined the odyssey.

"The new generation—you have to go out and discover," his father had told him before his death. "To be more lucky than us."

Abdoulaye knew America long before he got here. He knew the rhymes of Public Enemy and Tupac Shakur and the names of fashionable sneakers. He also knew how much money his compatriots had made here and taken back to Senegal.

Today, at 20, Abdoulaye is luckier than many of his peers. He lives with his uncles and their wives in the Bronx. He works at the family business, selling color televisions to fellow Africans. He just wasn't prepared for the loneliness.

In a palm-size photo album, he keeps snapshots of his friends back home. Abdoulaye misses their company terribly. On the subway, he listens to Youssou N'Dour on his headphones and writes to them, telling them the truth about this place they all once dreamed of. Recently, he wrote about attending his first American demonstration, in front of the house where Amadou Diallo died.

"You know, in my country, every time I walk the street, I was with one of my friends," he said. "Here, when I get out of school, I walk by myself. Nobody talks to me. I don't talk to nobody. I feel, 'Where I am? Where I am?'"

Monir calls home whenever he is blue, which is evidently often, considering he sometimes runs up a $200 phone bill. Often, the conversation turns to his future here, though, in typical immigrant fashion, he is less than candid about the fine points of his new life.

"I don't really tell them how much I work," he confided.

For a year and a half, he has worked seven hours a night, six nights a week at the Thai restaurant. At the end of each shift, he pockets $45.

His mother still presses him to come home, but so far, his more pragmatic parent has prevailed. "My father says, 'What is he going to do here?'" Monir explained.

More and more, he asks that same question of himself.

"I think a lot about whether to stay," he said, "or whether to go back."

LOW-WAGE EARNERS: TRAPPED IN POVERTY

Marcia Passos Duffy

The U.S. government sets the official poverty level based on estimated costs for food, housing, and other necessities. In the following article, however, Marcia Passos Duffy cites research revealing
that a family must earn more than twice the income established in
the government's guidelines in order to finance a modest standard
of living and escape poverty. Low-wage earners, who typically
make five or six dollars per hour, cannot earn enough to meet
their families' needs, she contends. According to the author, these
individuals are frequently unable to move into better-paying jobs
because there are too many workers competing for a limited number of available jobs, which enables employers to keep wages low.
Duffy is a freelance writer based in New England.

A family of four with an annual income of $16,985 is classified as liv-
ing below the poverty threshold set by the US government. But families that earn significantly more are also living in poverty, even
though they don't meet the government income guidelines, according to a recent report.

In fact, it takes a whole lot more than $16,985 to finance just a
modest standard of living, say researchers at the Economic Policy
Institute, a nonprofit economic think tank based in Washington,
D.C., which used some of the government's own figures in making
that assertion.

A second report, by the Community Service Society, a nonprofit
social advocacy group based in New York City, finds that hard times are
also hitting people who, historically, have been considered at low risk
for poverty, such as college-educated people and two-parent families.

According to the Economic Policy Institute's recent report, "How
Much is Enough?" a bare-bones budget for a family of four (two
adults and two children) ranges from $26,000 to $45,000 a year, more
than twice the poverty threshold.

"We were surprised how high (the budget numbers) added up,"

said policy analyst Chauna Brocht, who wrote the report with senior economist Jared Bernstein and policy analyst Maggie Spade-Aguilar. "These numbers don't even include credit card debt or provisions for savings or eating meals out."

Based on the income levels of these budgets, she added, few jobs in the low-wage sector of the labor market enable working families to meet their basic needs.

The Gap Between Pay and Basic Needs

The importance of these findings, Brocht said, is to point out the gap between the rates of pay available to many low-income workers and the amount required to meet basic needs. "Low-wage working parents making $5 or $6 an hour cannot earn enough to meet their families' basic needs, even with full-time work," she said. "There's a huge gap between the poor and the middle class in this country." Current median income for a US family of four is $56,000.

Low-income families tend to spend less on basic necessities than recommended by basic family budgets, a finding that suggests these families are not fully meeting their basic needs. "We believe the poverty line should be revised," Brocht said.

Researchers at New York City's Community Service Society agree, since more people—even some college educated—are tumbling into poverty. "People who you may not expect to be poor are becoming poor," said Mark Levitan, senior policy analyst. In a separate study, Levitan found that from the late 1980s to the late 1990s, poverty rates rose for the kinds of families that have traditionally had the least likelihood of living below the poverty line.

"In New York City, the archetypal poor has been the single mom on welfare with no job and no skills," said Levitan. While the majority of the poor in the city fit that stereotype, he noted, it is becoming less typical. "Now, alongside with the old definition of poverty, is the 'new poor.' I was shocked by this data."

According to the organization's study, which used the US Bureau of Census' annual report on income and poverty, the poverty rates for New York City families headed by an adult with some college climbed 10.6 percent in the past decade; poverty rates for families headed by a person with a bachelor's degree or more increased by 4 percent. Levitan said the data does not explain why some college-educated heads of households are not able to provide adequately for their families.

"Public policy has not done enough to cut a path out of poverty," Levitan said, but noted that the study was based on New York City's population, which has its own unique problems—including a large influx of immigrant workers and a large population of people who are now off the welfare rolls because of new federal restrictions on eligibility.

"In the low end of the labor market there are too many workers chasing too few jobs, keeping wages low," he said. Statewide, a proposal to raise the minimum wage from $5.15 an hour to $6.75 is gathering support, Levitan said.

In the short term, Brocht and Levitan believe that boosting the minimum wage and raising the minimum annual salary for families to be eligible for an earned income tax credit would offer some immediate relief. In the long term, Brocht suggested that the federal government look into subsidizing some basic needs, such as providing universal preschool free of charge to the neediest families.

In Maine, some benefits are already being linked to a "livable wage" that is calculated by what people actually have to spend to meet basic needs. That means that Mainers who earn less than the livable wage are eligible for some kinds of assistance, even if they earn more than minimum wage and their annual income is above the federal poverty line. Vermont is also considering this approach.

Levitan believes that training the low-wage workforce is the long-term answer. "The problem is that people get stuck in low-wage jobs and have no way of getting out."

A Breakdown of the No-Frills Budget

Here's a conservative, monthly no-frills budget calculated by the Economic Policy Institute, based on a family of four living in Baltimore. This budget does not include many "unnecessary" goods that most families take for granted, such as restaurant (even fast-food) meals, vacations, movies, savings for education and retirement, and emergency funds.

Food: $500 minimum for food prepared at home, as recommended by the US Department of Agriculture's low-cost food plan.

Housing: $628 for a two-bedroom apartment, as measured by the Department of Housing and Urban Development's fair market rents.

Health care: $267, an amount that recognizes that not all families receive health insurance through their employers.

Transportation: $222, for miles driven to work and other necessary trips. It is based on cost-per-mile estimates from the Internal Revenue Service.

Child care: $626 for center-based child care as reported by a local child care cost survey and in a Children's Defense Fund study.

Other necessary expenses: $338 for telephone, clothing, personal care, household items, bank fees, union dues, reading materials, school supplies and television, as reported in Consumer Expenditure Survey data.

Taxes: $313 for federal payroll taxes and federal, state and local income total. This expense also takes into account funds received through the earned income tax credit.

The grand total annual salary needed for a bare-bones budget for a family of four living in Baltimore: $34,732.28.

THE MYTH OF WIDESPREAD AMERICAN POVERTY

Robert Rector

Robert Rector is a senior policy analyst for welfare and poverty issues at the Heritage Foundation in Washington, D.C. In the following selection, he contends that reports from the U.S. Census Bureau overstate the extent of poverty in the United States and understate the real income of most Americans. Rector asserts that most people would define poverty as the lack of adequate food, clothing, or housing. Going by this definition, he states, only a few Americans are truly poor. In fact, the majority of those who are classified as impoverished by the Census Bureau are actually better housed, better fed, and own more property than the average American of just a few generations ago, Rector concludes.

In the last week of September 1998, the U.S. Census Bureau will issue its annual report on the number of Americans who are "living in poverty."

Census Bureau poverty reports vary little from year to year. For the past decade, the Census Bureau has declared that between 31.5 million and 39 million persons were living in poverty each year. In 1997, for example, the Census Bureau declared there were 36.5 million poor Americans—nearly 14 percent of the U.S. population. But a close look at the actual material living standards of persons defined as "poor" by the Census Bureau demonstrates that the Bureau's official poverty report is misleading. For most Americans, the word "poverty" means destitution, an inability to provide a family with nutritious food, adequate clothing, and reasonable shelter. But only a small number of the 36.5 million persons classified as "poor" by the Census Bureau fit such a description.

The Poor Are Better Off

In fact, numerous government reports indicate that most "poor" Americans today are better housed, better fed, and own more personal property than average Americans throughout most of the twentieth century. Today, inflation-adjusted expenditures per person among the lowest-income one-fifth (or quintile) of households equal those of the

Excerpted from "The Myth of Widespread American Poverty," by Robert Rector, *Heritage Foundation Backgrounder*, September 18, 1998. Copyright © 1998 by The Heritage Foundation. Reprinted with permission.

average American household in the early 1970s.

The following facts about persons defined as "poor" by the Census Bureau are taken from various government reports:

• In 1995, 41 percent of all "poor" households owned their own homes.

• The average home owned by a person classified as "poor" has three bedrooms, one-and-a-half baths, a garage, and a porch or patio.

• Over three-quarters of a million "poor" persons own homes worth over $150,000; and nearly 200,000 "poor" persons own homes worth over $300,000.

• Only 7.5 percent of "poor" households are overcrowded. Nearly 60 percent have two or more rooms per person.

• The *average* "poor" American has one-third more living space than the *average* Japanese does and four times as much living space as the *average* Russian.

• Seventy percent of "poor" households own a car; 27 percent own two or more cars.

• Ninety-seven percent have a color television. Nearly half own two or more televisions.

• Nearly three-quarters have a VCR; more than one in five has two VCRs.

• Two-thirds of "poor" households have air conditioning. By contrast, 30 years ago, only 36 percent of the entire U.S. population enjoyed air conditioning.

• Sixty-four percent of the "poor" own microwave ovens, half have a stereo system, and over a quarter have an automatic dishwasher.

• As a group, the "poor" are far from being chronically hungry and malnourished. In fact, poor persons are more likely to be overweight than are middle-class persons. Nearly half of poor adult women are overweight.

• Despite frequent charges of widespread hunger in the United States, 84 percent of the "poor" report their families have "enough" food to eat; 13 percent state they "sometimes" do not have enough to eat, and 3 percent say they "often" do not have enough to eat.

• The average consumption of protein, vitamins, and minerals is virtually the same for poor and middle-class children, and in most cases is well above recommended norms.

• Poor children actually consume more meat than do higher-income children and have average protein intakes that are 100 percent above recommended levels.

• Most poor children today are in fact super-nourished, growing up to be, on average, one inch taller and ten pounds heavier that the GIs who stormed the beaches of Normandy in World War II.

The Census Bureau counts as poor any household with cash income that is less than the official poverty threshold—which, in 1997, was $16,404 for a family of four. But the Census Bureau dramatically undercounts the incomes of these less affluent Americans. Other government surveys consistently show that spending by low-income households greatly exceeds the income the Census Bureau claims they have.

Why does this happen? Careful examination reveals that the annual Census poverty report dramatically exaggerates poverty and misrepresents the living conditions of lower-income Americans. The inaccuracy of the report is the result of three errors:

1. The Census Bureau deems that a family is "poor" if its annual cash income falls below certain specified "income thresholds." These thresholds were set in the early 1960s and have been raised upward in each subsequent year to adjust for inflation. For example, the poverty threshold for a family of four was roughly $3,100 in 1963 and reached $16,404 in 1997. This official poverty measurement served initially as a public relations instrument in President Lyndon Johnson's larger "War on Poverty." Therefore, the initial income thresholds were set artificially high in order to enlarge the apparent numbers of the poor and build public support for Johnson's welfare policies. Although families with incomes below the thresholds will face many financial difficulties, they are not necessarily poor in the sense of lacking adequate food, shelter, and clothing.

2. In determining whether a family is poor, the Census Bureau considers only current income and ignores all assets accumulated in prior years. Thus, a businessman who suffers temporary business losses resulting in a negative net income for the year will be labeled as "poor" even if he has a million dollars sitting in the bank.

3. The most critical error by far is that the Census radically undercounts the true economic resources or annual income received by the American public. This may be seen by comparing Census income figures with the U.S. Department of Commerce's National Income and Product Accounts (NIPA), which provide the figures measuring the gross national product (GNP). In 1996, NIPA figures show that aggregate "personal income" of Americans was $6.8 trillion. By contrast, aggregate personal income according to the Census Bureau's official definition of income was only $4.8 trillion. In other words, the Census missed $2 trillion in annual income, or roughly $20,000 for each U.S. household. The missing $2 trillion of personal income exceeds the entire economies of most of the world's nations. Much of the missing income belongs to the middle class and the rich; but low-income families receive a large slice as well.

The Condition of Households Classified as Poor

Spending and Income. In 1995, the Census Bureau claimed that the lowest income fifth (or quintile) of U.S. households had an average income of $8,350. In the same year, however, the Consumer Expenditure Survey of the U.S. Department of Labor showed that the average household, in the same lowest income quintile, spent $14,607.

The Labor Department and Census Bureau data directly contradict each other. The Labor Department survey shows $1.75 in spending for every $1.00 of income that the Census Bureau claims these same households possess. This is no fluke; a similarly wide gap between spending and alleged "income" occurred throughout the 1980s and 1990s.

But the picture is still incomplete. When counting household expenditures, the Labor Department's Consumer Expenditure Survey *excludes* public housing subsidies and health care subsidies provided through Medicaid, Medicare, and other government medical programs. If housing and medical subsidies are included, the total expenditures of the average household in the bottom income quintile rise to $20,335. This means that less affluent households spend $2.43 for every $1.00 of "income" reported by the Census Bureau.

Ownership of Property and Amenities. Some 41 percent of poor households actually own their own homes. The median value of homes owned by these households is $65,000, or 70 percent of the median value of all homes owned in America. Some 900,000 households, classified as poor, own homes worth over $150,000. The typical home owned by the "poor" is a three-bedroom house with one-and-a-half baths. It is in good repair, has a garage or carport, and was constructed in 1962. It has a porch or patio, and is located on a half-acre lot.

Roughly 70 percent of poor households own a car or truck. Remarkably, over one-fourth of poor households own two or more cars or trucks. Modern conveniences are very common and, in some cases, almost ubiquitous among poor households. Two-thirds of the poor have air conditioning; a similar number have microwaves, while almost 30 percent have automatic dishwashers.

It is not surprising that nearly all poor households have color television sets; but nearly half actually own two or more color television sets. Nearly three-fourths of the poor now have VCRs, and more than one in five own two VCRs. While these numbers do not suggest lives of luxury, they also seem quite distant from conventional images of poverty.

Housing Space

In the United States, both the overall population and the poor live, in general, in spacious housing. Nearly 70 percent of all U.S. households have two or more rooms per occupant. Among the poor overall, this figure is 60 percent. Among the urban poor, it is 55 percent. Crowding is quite rare; only 0.5 percent of all households and 1.9 percent of poor households are severely crowded, with 1.5 or more persons per room. Moderate crowding (1.01 to 1.50 persons per room) is slightly more common, characterizing 2.1 percent of all households and 5.6 percent of poor households.

Housing space also can be measured in square footage per person. At present, Americans have an average of 718 square feet of living space per person. Poor Americans have 440 square feet. By contrast, social reformer Jacob Riis—writing of tenement living conditions in New York City around 1890—described families living with four or five persons per room and some 20 square feet of living space per person.

International comparisons of living space can be instructive. The Housing Indicator Program conducted by the United Nations Centre for Human Settlements surveyed housing conditions in major cities in 54 different countries. The survey showed the United States to have, by far, the most spacious housing units, with 50 percent to 100 percent more square footage per capita than in other industrialized nations.

Although poor Americans do have less housing space than average Americans do, they compare quite favorably to the average population in most other nations. Housing space for poor Americans appears to be comparable to that of an average person living in Toronto, and greater than that of the average person living in Paris, London, or Vienna. Poor Americans have roughly twice the living space per person of the average citizen in middle-income countries, such as Greece or Poland. And poor American households have roughly four times more housing space per person than do the general populations of cities in the developing world, such as Cairo or Beijing.

Maintenance of Housing Units. Of course, it is possible that the housing of poor American households could be spacious and still dilapidated or unsafe. However, data from the American Housing Survey indicate that this is not the case. For example, the survey provides a tally of households with "severe physical problems." Only a tiny portion of poor households and an even smaller portion of total households fall into that category.

The most common "severe problem," according to the American Housing Survey, is a shared bathroom—when occupants lack a complete bathroom and must share bathroom facilities with individuals in a neighboring unit. This condition affects about one-half of 1 percent of all United States households and 2 percent of poor households. About 1 percent of all households and 2 percent of poor households have other "severe physical problems," of which the most common are repeated heating breakdowns and upkeep problems.

The American Housing Survey also provides a count of households affected by "moderate physical problems." A wider range of households fall into this category: nearly 9 percent of the poor and 5 percent of total households. However, the problems affecting these units are clearly modest. Although living in such units might be disagreeable by modern middle-class standards, they are a far cry from Dickens-like squalor. The most common problems are deficiencies in upkeep, the lack of a full kitchen, and the use of unvented oil, kerosene, or gas heaters as the household's primary heat source (the last condition occurs almost exclusively in the South).

Food Shortage and Hunger

There are frequent charges of widespread hunger and malnutrition in the United States. Reliable survey data show that while hunger definitely exists in the United States, it is relatively restricted in scope and frequency. For example, the Third National Health and Nutrition Examination Survey conducted by the U.S. Department of Health and Human Services in 1988–1989 found that 96 percent of U.S. households reported they had "enough food to eat." Some 3 percent reported that they "sometimes" did not have enough food, and around a half percent said they "often" did not have enough food. Among the poor, 84 percent reported having enough food, while 13.2 percent reported shortages "sometimes," and 2.7 percent "often."

Poverty and Food Quality. It is widely believed that lack of financial resources forces poor people to eat low-quality diets that are deficient in nutriments and high in fat. However, survey data show that nutriment density (amount of vitamins, minerals, and protein per 1,000 calories of food) does not vary by income class. Nor do the poor consume higher-fat diets than the middle class. Looking at a comparison of the percentage of calories derived from fat for low-income and high-income adult men and women, there is little variation by income level. The percentage with high fat intake (as a share of total calories) is virtually the same for low-income and upper-middle-income persons.

Poverty and Nutrition. The U.S. Department of Agriculture periodically surveys the food and nutriment consumption of American households. These surveys provide little evidence of widespread under-nutrition among the poor; in fact, they show that the average nutriment consumption among the poor closely resembles that of the upper middle class. Example: Children in families with incomes below the poverty level actually consume more meat than do children in families with incomes at 350 percent of poverty or higher (roughly $57,000 for a family of four in today's dollars).

The intake of nutriments (proteins, vitamins, and minerals) is very similar for poor and middle-class children, and is generally well above the recommended daily level. For example, the consumption of protein (a relatively expensive nutriment) among poor children is, on average, between 150 and 267 percent of the recommended daily allowance (RDA).

When shortfalls of specific vitamins and minerals appear (for example, among teenage girls), they tend to be very similar for the poor and the middle class. For example, while poor teenage girls, on average, tend to under-consume Vitamin E, Vitamin B-6, calcium, phosphorus, magnesium, iron, and zinc, a virtually identical under-consumption of these same nutriments appears among upper-middle-class teenage girls.

Overall, examination of the average nutriment consumption of

Americans reveals that age and gender play a far greater role in determining nutritional patterns than does income. The average nutriment intakes of adult women in the upper middle class (above 350 percent of poverty) more closely resemble the intakes of poor women than they do those of upper-middle-class men, children, or teens. The nutriment consumption of upper-middle-income preschoolers, as a group, is virtually identical to that of poor preschoolers, but not to the consumption of adults or older children in the upper middle class. This same pattern holds for adult males, teens, and most other age and gender groups.

It is important to note that the nutriment intake figures represent only the average nutriment intakes for poor children in various age categories. Thus, the figures do not necessarily rule out the possibility that there could be pockets of under-nutrition within each age group of poor children even while the average consumption of the group remains high. The data do, however, refute any claim of widespread under-nutrition and hunger among poor children in general.

Increase in Children's Size. During the twentieth century, improvements in nutrition and health have led to increases in the rate of growth and ultimate height and weight of American children. Poor children have been affected by this trend. Poor boys today at ages 18 and 19 are actually taller and heavier than similar aged boys in the general U.S. population in the late 1950s. Poor boys living today are one inch taller and some ten pounds heavier than GIs of similar age during World War II, and nearly two inches taller and 20 pounds heavier than American doughboys back in World War I.

This does not mean, of course, that all poor children have now reached optimal levels of health and nutrition. In particular, poor children remain more likely to be born at low birth weight than are children of higher income groups. Low birth weight, in turn, contributes to a slightly disproportionate number of poor children being short for their age, particularly in the preschool years. However, the general trend among poor children has been one of marked improvements in health and nutrition, leading to rapid growth and large stature.

Poverty and Obesity. The principal nutrition-related health problem among the poor, as with the general U.S. population, stems from over-consumption, not the under-consumption, of food. While overweight and obesity are prevalent problems throughout the United States, they are found most frequently among poor adults. Nearly half of poor adult women are overweight, compared with a third of women who are not poor.

Recently, health experts have expressed concern over the growing problem of obesity among children. Poor children have not been immune to this problem, and some studies actually have found obesity to be more prevalent among poor children than among middle-class children. For example, a 1993 pediatric study examined height and weight of school children aged 5 to 12 in inner-city Harlem. The children in the study were black or Hispanic, and nearly all were from low-income households. As a whole, these economically disadvantaged inner-city children were found to be above average in height and weight, compared with government norms. A large sub-group was markedly obese: The study noted that "more than a quarter of central Harlem children could be considered obese; of whom nearly 14% would be super obese." The authors noted the contrast between these inner-city children and the image of the lean black child that emerged from studies in the late 1960s.

Dr. Sue Kimm of the University of Pittsburgh used data from the Growth and Health Study (NGHS) of the National Heart, Lung, and Blood Institute to examine the relationship between obesity and socioeconomic status, based on a sample of nine- and ten-year-old girls drawn from Ohio, California, and the District of Columbia in 1987. The study found 19 percent of white girls and 31 percent of black girls were overweight. White girls from low-income families (below $10,000) were two to three times more likely to be overweight than were middle- and upper-income girls. The prevalence of obesity among blacks did not vary according to family income.

Few Are Impoverished

If poverty is defined as generally lacking adequate nutritious food for one's family, suitable clothing, and a reasonably warm, dry apartment in which to live, or lacking a car to get to work when one is needed, then there are few poor persons remaining in the United States. Real material hardship does occur in America, but it is limited in both extent and severity. The bulk of the "poor" live in material conditions that would have been judged comfortable or well-off just a few generations ago.

The old maxim that "the rich get richer and the poor get poorer" is simply untrue. Material conditions of lower-income Americans have improved dramatically over time. In fact, living conditions in the nation as a whole have improved so much that American society can no longer clearly remember what it meant to be poor or even middle class in earlier generations.

But higher material living standards should not be regarded as a victory for the War on Poverty. Living conditions were improving dramatically and poverty was dropping sharply long before the War on Poverty began. The principal effect of the War on Poverty has been not to raise incomes, but to displace self-sufficiency with dependence. A second consequence of welfare has been the destruction of families. When the War on Poverty began, 7.7 percent of children were born out of wedlock. Today, the figure is 32 percent. Using the Census Bureau's own standards, a child born to a never-married mother is

700 percent more likely to live in poverty than is a child born to a husband and wife whose marriage remains intact.

The Census poverty report has been tightly linked to the War on Poverty since its inception. The implicit message of the poverty report is that government should throw more and more welfare benefits at low-income communities in an effort to artificially raise family incomes above the official poverty thresholds. Such welfare policies have been disastrous.

Despite spending $7 trillion, the War on Poverty—by eroding the work ethic and marriage—has failed. By undermining families' capacity for self-support, the War on Poverty expanded the clientele of needy persons. Government became caught in a trap: The more aid that it gave, the more persons in apparent need of its aid emerged. With the Welfare Reform Act of 1996, the federal government finally began to break away from this failed entitlement mentality. But the Census Bureau report continues to embody the old, failed philosophy of unending free handouts.

Poverty and Social Problems

The Census poverty report also has had a distorting effect on the national dialogue by focusing attention exclusively on income and material living standards while ignoring values and behavior. The report is rooted in the belief that "poverty" causes social problems such as crime, drug use, school failure, illegitimacy, and dependence. This belief, although common, is false. Clearly, there were far more truly poor persons in earlier generations than there are today. (In fact, nearly all adults alive today had parents or grandparents who grew up "poor" in the sense of having incomes below the current Census thresholds, adjusted for inflation.) If it were true that "poverty" causes social and behavioral problems, then earlier generations should have been awash in drugs, crime, and promiscuity. But this was not the case. Most social problems have *expanded* as incomes have increased.

In reality, it is the norms and values within a family, rather than its income, that are critical to a child's well-being and prospects for success in future life. Ironically, conventional welfare, with its misplaced emphasis on artificially boosting income, has a strongly damaging effect on the very values that are critical to a child's success. By ignoring values and undermining the norms of work, self-control, and marital stability, the War on Poverty has harmed those whom it intended to help.

Overall, the Census poverty report is deeply flawed as a measurement tool and misleading as a policy indicator. The report not only exaggerates poverty, but, even more tragically, encourages policymakers to focus on the symptom of income shortage while ignoring behavioral problems, which are the root causes of the lack of income. As such, the report serves both society and the poor badly.

CHAPTER 2

THE CAUSES OF INNER-CITY POVERTY

VARIOUS THEORIES ON THE CAUSES OF POVERTY

Harrell R. Rodgers Jr.

In the following excerpt from his book *American Poverty in a New Era of Reform*, Harrell R. Rodgers Jr. explains that researchers have proposed different—and sometimes conflicting—theories for why poverty exists. He presents two major categories of theories concerning poverty: cultural/behavioral and structural/economic. According to the author, proponents of cultural/behavioral theories generally argue that poverty is rooted in the conduct and values of the poor. These theories maintain that poor people are prone to behaviors or beliefs—such as substance abuse or a poor work ethic—that limit their ability to improve their lot. On the other hand, Rodgers notes, proponents of structural/economic theories maintain that poverty is caused by factors outside of poor people's control, including racial discrimination and a shortage of economic opportunities in inner-city areas. He also points out that poverty may be caused by a complex interplay of both cultural/behavioral and structural/economic problems.

Why do we have poverty in a country as rich as America? While many people, including some scholars, seem to think the answer is simple, a thoughtful analysis suggests that the antecedents of poverty are quite complex. The first complication is that the poverty population is much more diverse than many people imagine. The poverty population is an elaborate mix of people who vary by age, race, sex, geographic location, and family structure. The poor are generally stereotyped as primarily single women and their children, illegitimate or otherwise, along with street people. But, among the poor can be found the elderly, often living alone, married-couple families with children in which one or sometimes even both parents are employed, young healthy males who may or may not be in the labor force, single or married adults without children, and farm workers following crop rotations across the nation. The poor can be found in every state, in central cities, in suburbs and rural areas in every region of the nation.

Does it seem reasonable that the same factor or factors are responsible for the poverty of all these diverse groups of people? Is an eighty-five-year-old widow poor for the same reasons as an eighteen-year-old single mother or an alcoholic derelict?

The Most Common Mistake

Not likely. The most common mistake in thinking about the causes of poverty is to generalize based on one group among the poor. If we think that poverty is basically only a problem related to teenagers having children out-of-wedlock, or adults who abuse alcohol or drugs, we are not likely to ever understand the complexities of the broader problem well enough to fashion creative solutions. Our understanding, or even biases, about the causes of poverty have a significant impact on the type of solutions we are willing to support. Many people who might be willing to sanction adults who refuse to work or teenage mothers who will not attend parenting classes would likely have a very different attitude about a parent who worked full-time but could not escape poverty. It is important, therefore, to achieve as sophisticated an understanding as possible of the causes of poverty.

When all the various types of people who are poor are examined, it becomes obvious that poverty is not a single problem, but rather a series of problems that affect diverse groups within our population. Additionally, being poor does not automatically mean that a person is a welfare recipient. Only some of the poor receive welfare. For a variety of reasons many poor people never apply for assistance, and others would find qualifying for aid to be quite difficult because most assistance is reserved for select groups of poor people. Stereotypes of the poor often result from the fact that only some of the poor receive the cash benefits that society thinks of as welfare. Those people who qualify for cash assistance—mostly female-headed families—tend to be thought of as the poor. But they are really a subset of the poor.

Even being cognizant of the diversity and complexity of poverty and the use of welfare by the poor will not solve all our analytical problems. Fashioning public policies to solve poverty would certainly be easier if there was agreement about the causes of poverty. But even when we examine the poverty of a particular person or a specific group of people, individual values impact perceptions of why these people are poor. Think about this example. The poverty rate for married-couple families with children is rather low—about 7 percent. A number of seemingly rather obvious factors make a rather small percentage of these families poor. Some of these families, for example, go through periods of unemployment, and some work full-time but receive very low wages, a not uncommon problem in many central cities and rural areas. Some family heads suffer illness, or become disabled, perhaps because of a job-related injury.

While the basic reasons these families suffer poverty may seem clear, there are many ways to diagnose their problems. If unemployment is a problem, how did the parents become unemployed? Did they fail to take employment seriously? Did they have the misfortune of being downsized? Do the parents abuse alcohol or drugs? Have the parents remained unemployed because they refuse to accept jobs they consider undesirable? Are they willing to relocate to an area with more jobs? Are both parents seeking employment? Is one parent forced to stay home because child care is too high or unavailable? Are the parents at fault for having children despite their low income potential? Have the parents been wronged by employers who fail to offer adequate benefits (e.g., health care or day care) or exhibit too little concern about the on-job safety of their employees?

Depending upon individual values and perhaps the behavior of the individuals involved, there are considerable grounds for differences in perspectives about why these families are poor, whether they should be offered any assistance, and, if so, what type of assistance they should be given. The same is true, of course, for other subgroups of the poor. Thus, agreeing on the causes of poverty is quite difficult. . . .

Theories of Poverty

Theories of poverty generally fall into one of two categories: cultural/behavioral or structural/economic. Structural/economic theories usually contain some behavioral component, but argue that the precipitating factor that causes poverty is a lack of equal opportunities for all Americans. Cultural/behavioral theories generally make the case that the only real cause of poverty is the behavior, values, and culture of the poor. Conservatives generally favor cultural/behavioral arguments, while moderates and liberals usually emphasize structural/ economic explanations that contain a behavioral component.

Cultural/Behavioral Theories. In *The Dream and The Nightmare,* Myron Magnet articulates a conservative interpretation of American poverty. Magnet argues that the basic cause of poverty is the culture and behavior of the poor. People become poor, Magnet argues, not because they lack social, political, and economic opportunities, but because they lack the inner resources to seize the ample opportunities that surround them. Magnet believes the poverty of the poor is primarily a destitution of the soul, a failure to develop the habits of education, reasoning, judgment, sacrifice, and hard work required to succeed in the world. To Magnet the poor are not hardworking, decent people who have fallen victim to economic problems. Rather, he says, they are people who engage in school-leaving, welfare abuse, illegitimacy, drug and alcohol abuse, and often crime.

The primary job of any civilization, Magnet says, is soulcraft: the transmission of values which combine to develop mature, educated, honest, hardworking, caring, and responsible people. The poor represent society's failures, those who have not inherited the central values of mainstream culture. Magnet believes that the values of today's poor reflect the revolutionized culture of the 1960s, which taught that it was legitimate to blame the system for personal failures and expect government handouts rather than seek success through education, hard work, and sacrifice. This same 1960s culture also promoted the sexual revolution, endorsing premarital sex, promiscuity, and illegitimacy, while degrading marriage, sacrifice, education, and industriousness.

Magnet's concluding point is that an individual's values and behavior determines his/her opportunities, economic or otherwise. Economic opportunity can abound, but if a person lacks the inner resources to take advantage of opportunities, he/she will fail. Giving welfare to those who fail only makes matters worse. Welfare reinforces the belief that people are not responsible for their behavior, that they cannot overcome their problems through hard work, and that welfare is something they deserve.

A Narrowly Drawn Stereotype

Moderate and liberal scholars tend to believe that the image of the poor drawn by Magnet and others who accept his point of view is nothing but a narrowly drawn stereotype. This view of the poor, they argue, is based on a subset of the poor, which ignores the complexity of the poverty population and empirical evidence about length of poverty spells and welfare use. Out of a population of 35 to 40 million poor people, Magnet, they argue, bases his theory of poverty on the behavior and welfare use of a few million of the poor, a group often labeled the underclass. Those poor people with obviously dysfunctional habits or lifestyles have long interested society. Often they have been labeled as the undeserving poor, or more recently as the underclass. But what proportion of the poor do they represent?

A considerable body of research has attempted to define and identify the underclass. Scholars who have attempted to identify and count them have used a number of definitions and methodologies. Some studies have tried to define the underclass as those poor who are isolated in inner-city impoverished neighborhoods, essentially separated from the workforce. These studies identify a rather small underclass population ranging from under 1 million to about 6 million.

Another group of scholars have tried to identify those long-term poor people, often including those who live in neighborhoods with high concentrations of poverty, who engage in dysfunctional behavior such as chronic unemployment, drug use, out-of-wedlock births, crime, school-leaving, and antisocial attitudes and behavior. These studies identify a population that ranges from less than 1 million to slightly more than 8 million, depending upon definitions, methodologies, and number of cities studied.

While these various studies arrive at estimates that differ considerably, they do agree that most of the poor are not the highly dysfunc-

tional people described by Magnet. That proportion of the poor population that does exhibit serious social problems, however, is considerable, quite visible, and they are expensive users of social services. It is
not too surprising that this group is often thought of as the poor.

A Flawed Welfare System?

Many conservative scholars, on the other hand, are not concerned
about stereotyping the poor because they think Magnet's basic arguments are both correct and should serve as a warning. They believe
that the welfare system is so perverse in design that it has the ability
to spread a contagion of pathologies among the poor. Charles Murray
in his influential book *Losing Ground* argued that the real culprit of
the poor is welfare. Welfare, Murray argues, robs the poor of initiative,
breaks up families by encouraging men either not to marry the mothers of their children or to desert them, provides an incentive to
women to have children out-of-wedlock, so they can get on welfare or
increase their benefits, and discourages work by providing a combination of cash and noncash benefits that amounts to better compensation than could be obtained through employment.

Murray's arguments have attracted strong critics, in part, because
he proposes a radical solution. Murray argues that the best way to
reduce poverty is simply to abolish all welfare programs. Labeled the
cold turkey approach, Murray's arguments are almost the perfect foil
for those sympathetic towards the poor. But even critics of Murray
often agree that welfare does produce some antifamily impacts.
Researchers Sheldon Danziger, David T. Ellwood and Mary Jo Bane,
and Lauri Jo Bassi all found a significant link between welfare receipt
and increased rates of divorce. Irwin Garfinkel and Sara S. McLanahan
concluded that while welfare receipt often delays remarriage, it has a
modest impact on divorce and out-of-wedlock births.

Also, there is little relationship between state Aid to Families with
Dependent Children (AFDC) benefits and state out-of-wedlock birth
rates. The out-of-wedlock birth rate, in other words, is not higher in
states that pay high AFDC benefits than the rate in states that pay low
benefits. In fact, Mississippi, one of the lowest-paying states in the
nation, has one of the highest out-of-wedlock birth rates. Critics like
Murray countered that the amount of the state grant is less important
than the fact that an out-of-wedlock birth makes a women eligible for
welfare or may increase her benefits, even modestly. Murray argues
that if states gave no money to single mothers, especially teenagers,
parents would put more pressure on teenagers to avoid pregnancy,
and women would expect more of men—and would be more careful
about having children with men who did not have the prospect of
becoming parental partners.

Other scholars take a somewhat different approach than Murray,
but argue that welfare programs play an important role in making

and keeping people poor. In a pair of influential books, Lawrence M. Mead argued that the welfare system had become too permissive, placing too few obligations on the recipients. By not requiring the healthy poor to work, Mead contended, the welfare system undermined both the confidence of the poor and public sympathy for them. One of Mead's theses was that passive poverty, that is an idle poverty population, reflected a welfare-nurtured defeatism on the part of recipients rather than a real lack of economic opportunity. Mead focused, first, on proving that the healthy poor could work and, second, on documenting ample economic opportunity for those with motivation. Mead argued that the poor would be substantially better off economically and psychologically if they were moved into the workforce and that society would be much more positive about helping low-income working families than in assisting passive welfare families. Thus, Mead did not contend that all welfare is wrong or harmful, but rather that welfare, especially long-term, is the wrong solution to the problems of the healthy poor.

James L. Payne agrees with the fundamental position of conservatives that welfare is harmful to the poor. Payne makes the familiar argument that welfare destroys the integrity of the poor while promoting and prolonging poverty by asking too little in return. Payne advocates what he calls "expectant giving," basing most assistance to the poor on the understanding that they must give something in return. "What the poor actually need," argues Payne, "is to be asked to give, not be given to." "Expectant giving" requires the poor to engage in constructive efforts to help themselves. The best assistant programs, Payne argues, are those that require the greatest contribution from the poor.

Payne takes the conservative argument one step further. He contends that government can never pass or administer effective welfare reform. The reason, he argues, is that governments will always yield to a handout mentality, based on the belief that the poor, regardless of why they are poor, deserve help. "Expectant giving" requires judgments about why people are poor, what they need, what they should give in return, and whether they have lived up to the terms of their agreement or contract. Effectively helping the poor, Payne argues, requires that they be treated selectively or unequally, a role government is unsuited to play. With heavy caseloads, endless, inflexible rules, and a bias toward uniformity, government programs, he says, will always drift to handouts. The best alternative, Payne suggests, is to turn welfare over to private, voluntary efforts that can be more flexible and creative. Only then, says Payne, can we avoid the extremes of indulgence and cruelty that exacerbate America's poverty problems.

The cultural/behavioral approach, in summary, basically places responsibility for America's poverty problem on the personal inadequacies of the poor, welfare in general, or the design flaws of welfare programs.

Examining Urban Black Ghettos

Structural/Economic Theories. As noted, moderates and liberals generally explain poverty in terms of limited economic or political opportunities, changes in government policies, and sometimes racial and/or sexual discrimination. An important theory offered by William J. Wilson in *The Truly Disadvantaged* examines the impact of civil rights laws on changes in economic opportunities. Wilson's theory focuses on the growth of poverty and social problems in urban black ghettos. Blacks, Wilson notes, migrated from the South to the major cities of the Midwest and North in search of economic opportunities. Because of housing discrimination, almost all black people, regardless of education or skills, became concentrated in central city ghettos. By the 1970s, Wilson maintains, important changes were taking place in American society that would have major impacts on black ghettos. Wilson explains these dynamics with four hypotheses.

First, Wilson hypothesizes that changes in the employment market harmed low-income, low-skilled blacks, especially black men living in central cities. These changes involved the general decline of manufacturing jobs, which paid good wages for low-skill work, and the migration of hundreds of thousands of these same types of manufacturing jobs from central cities to the suburbs. Replacing these manufacturing jobs in the central cities were clerical and white-collar jobs. However, these jobs tended to require more postsecondary or specialized skills than many ghetto residents possessed. Wilson labels these changes as slow economic growth, skills mismatch, and spatial mismatch. Slow economic growth reduced the number of manufacturing jobs; the jobs that increased in urban areas were those that many poor blacks were unqualified to fill, while those jobs they could perform were increasingly located in suburbs.

Second, Wilson hypothesizes that increased joblessness among inner-city men encouraged many of them to turn to idleness and hustling, including criminal activities such as the drug trade. The combination of unemployment and crime among so many men left ghetto women with fewer qualified or desirable partners, significantly reducing the marriage rate while increasing the incidence of out-of-wedlock births and the use of welfare.

Third, the civil rights laws passed in the 1960s played an important role in making these problems worse. Civil rights and affirmative action laws extending equal employment opportunities and fair housing increased the income of the most educated and skilled ghetto residents and allowed them to move to the suburbs. Wilson calls this selective out-migration.

Fourth, Wilson theorizes that selective out-migration harmed the ghetto community in important ways. Those who migrated had been the communities' best role models and civic leaders. Gone were those community leaders who had championed the importance of education, quality schools, and high academic standards while resisting crime and illegitimacy. In turn, those left behind had less education, skill, and motivation. This produced what Wilson labels a contagion effect, the degeneration of aspirations, morals, schools, and the general health of the community—leading to ever-increasing rates of poverty and other social problems.

Wilson's theory is interesting and important because it provides a tightly reasoned theory of the growth of the black underclass in American ghettos. Wilson emphasizes a loss of low-skilled, decent paying jobs as the precipitating event in increasing poverty in ghettos, but there is also a behavioral component. Wilson does not deny that many poor people engage in behaviors that make and keep them poor. He believes, however, that economic problems set off the chain of events that increased poverty and social problems in central cities.

Opposing Views

Wilson's theory has attracted opposition on two points. First, some scholars condemn Wilson, a black scholar, because he places no emphasis on racial discrimination as a cause of ghetto poverty. Wilson, in fact, believes that racism plays a declining role in black poverty. Other scholars have argued that racism is the primary reason for the increasing marginalization of black males. Second, other scholars fault Wilson for not crediting welfare with making any real contribution to ghetto poverty. Scholars such as Mead, Murray, and Payne, of course, believe that welfare played a pivotal role. Mead criticizes Wilson's theory by pointing out that low-skill immigrants have a history of maintaining high employment levels, often doing so despite language barriers. Mead believes that immigrants sustain high employment levels because they were not raised in welfare families. Blacks, on the other hand, Mead says, often grew up in or around welfare families and are, therefore, more willing to turn to welfare rather than accept low-paying jobs that they consider unpleasant, demeaning, or unrewarding or obtain the education or job skills required for better employment.

Welfare and Poverty

Mickey Kaus in *The End of Equality* takes a somewhat different position. Kaus argues that welfare might not be the actual cause of poverty, but that it is the welfare system that sustains it. Kaus raises the question of why ghetto blacks did not follow low-skill jobs as they moved to the suburbs. Wilson's answer is that for many ghetto residents the jobs, once increased transportation and housing costs were factored in, do not pay enough to make them feasible. Kaus finds that answer suspect. He notes that blacks left the South in large numbers and traveled long distances in search of employment opportunities, but they often failed to follow jobs as they moved to the suburbs. Why, asks Kaus, did they travel a thousand miles to seek improved economic opportunities but fail to follow jobs that were 25 miles away? His answer is welfare. Blacks migrated from the south, he says, because they had no choice. The welfare system did not exist and was not an option. However, when urban jobs migrated to the suburbs, black citizens often had an option. Rather than follow the jobs, they could qualify for welfare and become idle. And, that, Kaus says, is exactly what many of them did.

There is empirical evidence to support some of Wilson's hypotheses. Considerable research supports Wilson's skills-mismatch and spatial mismatch hypotheses. John D. Kasarda and J.H. Johnson and M.L. Oliver have documented the recent loss of decent paying manufacturing jobs to the suburbs, especially in the major cities of the Northeast and North-Central regions. Harry J. Holzer found that when jobs left the central cities for the suburbs, blacks lost more jobs and employment opportunities than did whites or suburban blacks. Research also documents a general decline in the wages of low-income workers. Since the mid-1970s wage increases have primarily taken place only in jobs that require higher levels of skill and education.

The empirical literature provides no support for Wilson's hypothesis that lack of economic opportunity explains the declining black marriage rate. The marriage rate for blacks has been declining at least since the 1950s, and seems to be little impacted by fluctuating black male employment levels, or the skill-level, education, or income of black males. As we will note below, Cornel West has a completely different explanation for the decline in black marriage rates.

Wilson's out-migration hypothesis is generally supported by empirical research. Wilson's contagion hypothesis has not been rigorously tested, but there is some evidence in support. Christopher Jencks and S. Mayer found that peers significantly affect academic achievement. Students perform better when they attend schools with peers who take education seriously and perform at higher levels. Saul D. Hoffman, Greg J. Duncan, and Ronald B. Mincy found that the higher the proportion of single welfare mothers in a neighborhood, the higher the rate of teenage pregnancy. Elijah Anderson, R.L. Jarret, and Jeffrey Fagan all found that young ghetto men turn to hustling when good jobs are unavailable.

In summary, much of Wilson's theory is supported by empirical and ethnographic research, although the role that welfare and racism do, or do not play, is seriously contested, and there is little support for the marriage hypothesis.

Another prominent black scholar offers a structural theory of black poverty, which includes some of the fundamentals of Wilson's theory.

Wilson basically believes that black poverty stems from economic problems, and he believes that economic reform would go a long way toward reducing the poverty and social problems of the ghetto. But Cornel West in his book *Race Matters* argues that while there is an economic antecedent, the problems of the black population are more complex than Wilson imagines. West agrees with Wilson that many black people, especially those who live in central city ghettos, engage in self-destructive behavior. But West argues that this dysfunctional behavior has complicated antecedents, reflecting problems not just of the economy, but also of America's culture, and, thus, cannot be reversed simply by economic reform.

West attributes the poverty and social problems of poor blacks to four factors:

- First, the economic decline that has taken place within the inner cities of America and the change in compensation for low-skilled jobs. His analysis of economic problems that have harmed the black population is very similar to Wilson's.

- Second, a history of racism along with continuing discrimination that West believes has done great emotional harm to millions of black people.

- Third, a prevailing American culture that stresses materialism and material gain to the exclusion of other, more important values, especially intellectual, moral, and spiritual growth. Materialism, West argues, is such a dominant value in American society that it is the core of American culture. As such, says West, it should be admitted that this perverse culture is a form of structure, much like the economy and the political system. When mainstream culture is so shallow that it reflects primarily market moralities, he argues, it misdirects and teaches low value, thus keeping people from becoming fully developed, successful humans with culture and meaningful values.

- Fourth, a lack of quality black leadership. West is extremely critical of black leadership, arguing that most black leaders are unprepared to transcend narrow racial issues, be examples of moral and spiritual growth, and lead with real vision and courage.

West believes that the combination of base cultural values, racism (past and present), economic problems, and poor leadership has produced battered identities in much of black America. These battered identities express themselves in two ways. First, West contends, many black people suffer from nihilism, a disease of the soul that manifests itself by producing lives of "horrifying meaninglessness, hopelessness, and (most important) lovelessness. . . . Life without meaning, hope, and love," West concludes, "breeds a cold-hearted, mean-spirited outlook that destroys both the individual and others." Second, is racial reasoning. Racial reasoning, West says, is not moral reasoning. "The humanity of black people," says West, "does not rest on deifying or demonizing others." Racial reasoning leads to a closing-ranks mentality that takes the form of inchoate xenophobia (poorly thought out fears and dislikes about foreigners), systematic sexism (which West says contributes significantly to the declining black marriage rate), and homophobia.

West believes that racial reasoning must be replaced with moral reasoning, which would produce mature black identities, coalition strategies that cross race lines, and black cultural democracy. Mature blacks could be honest about themselves and other black people, would be willing to work with other groups to achieve collective goals, and would promote a society in which black people treated everyone with respect, regardless of race, ethnicity, sex, or sexual orientation.

West's recommended solutions go beyond reducing black poverty, and they can be summarized in four parts. First, West believes that black people need a love ethic that would confront the self-destructive and inhumane actions of black people. Second, black people, he says, must also understand that the best source of help, hope, and power is themselves. The combined power of mature blacks must be focused on the public square. Black people, in other words, must participate in the debate, shaping, and passage of enlightened public policies designed to advance good values and stable, prosperous families. Third, government programs to aid low-income and poor people must be increased. And last, there needs to be a new generation of black leadership with genuine vision and courage and a commitment to uphold ethical and religious ideas.

West's theory is provocative and challenging. He is basically arguing that just improving the economic opportunities will not solve the fundamental problems of millions of black people. He believes that millions of poor blacks suffer from battered identities, destructive reasoning, perverse cultural values, and inadequate black leadership. Solving the problems of many poor blacks, he argues, requires an alteration in the basic values of our culture, along with enlightened public policies and better leadership. . . .

What These Theories Reveal

What insights do we gain from this review of theories? There are several and they are important. First, poverty is not a single problem; it is a series of rather complex problems. There are both cultural/behavioral and structural/economic causes of poverty, which vary by the subgroups of people found among the poor. Culture and structure are also connected. Opportunities influence culture, which influences behavior, which influences opportunity, which influences culture, ad infinitum.

Even when the same set of factors cause poverty, the problem of poverty varies because of the differential reactions of those who become poor. Some single mothers, for example, might seize the chance to obtain job training, and transitional health and child care to allow them to enter the workforce, while others may use every excuse possible to avoid accepting responsibility for themselves. Therefore, both variations in causes and reactions to poverty make the problem complex.

Second, the economy is important. The economy must be kept healthy and growing to provide quality opportunities for low-income and poor people. Third, many families cannot take advantage of economic opportunities without a better education or advanced job training. Fourth, similarly, many of today's poor people, especially parents, cannot work without child care and healthcare assistance. Fifth, some people will need extra help, encouragement, even sanction, to make the transition to employment. These people will need not only education and skill training, but also help with interpersonal skills, self-esteem, hope, and confidence before they believe in themselves enough and interact with others well enough to benefit from assistance and become self-sufficient. Some people will need help more than once. When they fail, they will need a second or even third push to get on their feet. Some people will need assistance in overcoming alcohol and drug dependency problems before they can be helped into the job market.

Sixth, discrimination based on sex, race, or ethnicity cannot be tolerated. Assistance programs and the employment market must be free of bias. Last, poverty, especially among the elderly, would be greatly reduced if the government sponsored more programs designed to help people save during their employment years.

THE ECONOMIC FACTORS BEHIND LONG-TERM POVERTY

Rebecca M. Blank

Rebecca M. Blank is the author of *It Takes a Nation: A New Agenda for Fighting Poverty*, from which the following selection is excerpted. She writes that there are two types of poor people: those who experience a brief spell of poverty and then move up the economic ladder, and those who never seem able to escape living in poverty. According to the author, people become poor either because of a change in the composition of the family (such as when a divorce results in a dramatic decline in total household income) or because the head of the household experiences a major decrease in earnings (due to extended unemployment or similar causes). More families fall into poverty due to the second reason, Blank reports, and an increase in earnings is often the factor that enables families to leave poverty.

We care not only about *who* is poor and *why* they are poor, but also how long they are poor. People who are poor for only one or two years might be considered less disadvantaged than those who are poor year after year. Those among the poor we worry about the most are those who seem unable to escape poverty. This group may be experiencing the most sustained effects of poverty, through accumulated health problems, long-term inadequate housing, and lack of access to or experience in the mainstream labor market. The long-term poor also use the most government resources and are therefore the most expensive from a taxpayer's point of view.

When we discuss the duration of poverty, we can present the picture in two quite different ways. On the one hand, most people who become poor are not poor for very long. On the other hand, there is a substantial minority of poor persons who seem to be poor for extremely long periods of time. How can both of these statements be true? Let's take a random sample of Americans and follow them over thirteen years to see how many were poor most of those years, some of those years, or none of those years.

Years of Poverty Among Americans

Figure 1 shows the number of years of poverty experienced among a random sample of Americans whose income was surveyed annually over the years 1979 to 1991. For thirteen recent years, these data indicate how prevalent poverty is and how much it is concentrated in long and short spells.

Two-thirds of all persons are never in a poor family during these thirteen years. About half of those who are ever poor are poor for only one to three years. Only 1.5 percent of the population is poor all thirteen years, but 5 percent are poor for ten or more years.

Of course, among different groups, these numbers look quite different. For whites, poverty is much more likely to be short term, while for blacks the duration of poverty is longer. Figure 2 shows how the extent of poverty differs among blacks and whites between 1979 and 1991. While only one-fourth of whites ever experience poverty in one of these years, almost two-thirds of all blacks experience at least one year of poverty. Furthermore, among white families who experience poverty, two-thirds are poor for only three years or less; barely 2 percent are poor ten years or more. In sharp contrast, a shocking 17 percent of the black population is poor for ten or more of these thirteen years.

These data suggest that differences in annual poverty rates between African Americans and white Americans *understate* the differences in economic need among these two groups. Black Americans are not only more likely to be poor at any point in time, but they are much more likely to be poor for long periods of time, suffering the cumulative effects of continuing poverty. Continuous, long-term poverty might be a particular concern among children. If we look only at children who

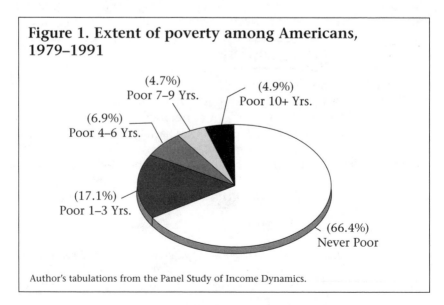

Figure 1. Extent of poverty among Americans, 1979–1991

(4.7%) Poor 7–9 Yrs.
(4.9%) Poor 10+ Yrs.
(6.9%) Poor 4–6 Yrs.
(17.1%) Poor 1–3 Yrs.
(66.4%) Never Poor

Author's tabulations from the Panel Study of Income Dynamics.

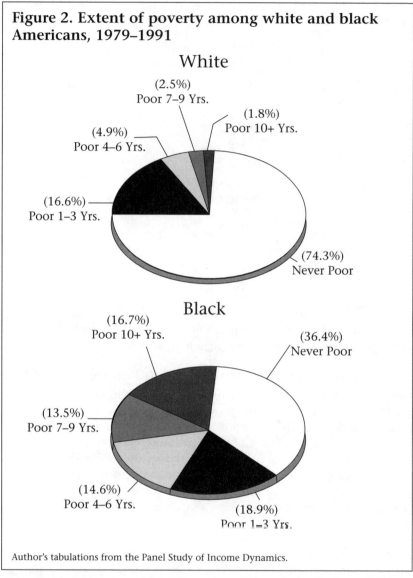

Figure 2. Extent of poverty among white and black
Americans, 1979–1991

White

(2.5%)
Poor 7–9 Yrs.

(1.8%)
Poor 10+ Yrs.

(4.9%)
Poor 4–6 Yrs.

(16.6%)
Poor 1–3 Yrs.

(74.3%)
Never Poor

Black

(16.7%)
Poor 10+ Yrs.

(36.4%)
Never Poor

(13.5%)
Poor 7–9 Yrs.

(14.6%)
Poor 4–6 Yrs.

(18.9%)
Poor 1–3 Yrs.

Author's tabulations from the Panel Study of Income Dynamics.

were eight or younger in 1980, a tiny proportion of white children
(less than 3 percent) is poor for ten or more of the next thirteen years.
But over 32 percent of black children are poor for that time.

Perhaps to no one's surprise, those groups most likely to be poor at
any point in time are also more likely to be poor over time. One
exception to this is the elderly. While overall poverty rates among the
elderly are relatively low, when an elderly person becomes poor, he or
she typically remains poor for the rest of his or her life.

The long-term poor are more likely to be African American, as we
have seen, to have low levels of education, to report health problems,

Figure 3. Reasons why poverty spells begin

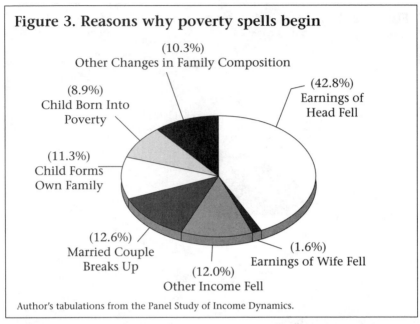

(10.3%)
Other Changes in Family Composition

(8.9%)
Child Born Into
Poverty

(42.8%)
Earnings of
Head Fell

(11.3%)
Child Forms
Own Family

(12.6%)
Married Couple
Breaks Up

(1.6%)
Earnings of Wife Fell

(12.0%)
Other Income Fell

Author's tabulations from the Panel Study of Income Dynamics.

or to be in single-mother families. Those who are least able to support themselves through earnings are also least able to escape poverty.

What Causes Poverty and How Do People Escape?

There is clearly a great deal of fluidity among the poor population. Many people enter and leave poverty each year. How does this happen? By looking at the changing circumstances that lead families to become poor and to escape poverty, we may gain some insight into the problems that poor families face and how they solve them.

We can follow each person in our random sample of the U.S. population over the same thirteen-year period from 1979 to 1991 and identify the family and economic changes that are associated with the beginning of all observed spells of poverty between these years. (Those who never became poor or who were poor in all years obviously do not contribute any information to this calculation.) Similarly, we can also look at the events that occur when people escape poverty for all spells of poverty that end between these years. I assume that changes in marital and family status are of first importance in explaining why a spell of poverty begins or ends. Thus, even though there is often a sharp decline in earnings in families after a divorce when the husband (and his earnings) leaves and the wife becomes the head of the family, I list the cause of poverty in this case as "married couple breaks up." Only in families where the same person is the head of the family for two years in a row can "earnings of head (of family) fell" be the cause of poverty.

Figure 3 shows how people enter poverty. In about one-quarter of the cases, a person enters poverty when there is a major change in his or her family composition—either a married couple breaks up, or a child who was living with his or her parents establishes an independent household. In another 10 percent of cases there are changes in family composition other than a change in the family head; for instance, an unmarried sibling who contributed earnings to the family might move out. In 9 percent of the cases, a person is born into a poor family. But in the majority of cases, poverty starts for a person when the economic situation of his or her family changes, with no changes in family composition. Almost half of all poverty spells start when the earnings of either the head or the wife fall, and another 12 percent start when other income sources are lost, such as a decline in child support, public assistance, or pension income.

In short, there are two main reasons why people become poor: either their families change composition in ways that threaten their economic security, or there is a major economic loss (usually in earnings). Most of these are job losses, where family heads experience extended unemployment. Among these two reasons, changes in economics create more poverty than changes in family composition.

Figure 4 shows equivalent information on how and why an individual leaves poverty. Over two-thirds of poor people escape poverty when a change occurs in their family's economic resources. In the majority of cases, poverty ends because either the earnings of the head or the wife increase enough to escape poverty, although increases in other income (typically government assistance) ends 16 percent of

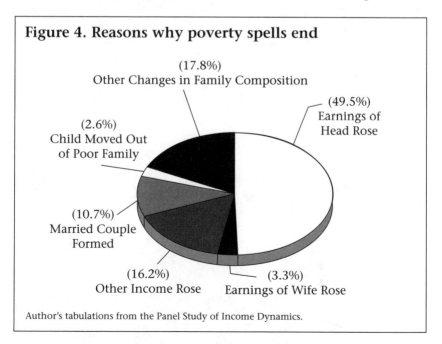

Figure 4. Reasons why poverty spells end

(17.8%)
Other Changes in Family Composition

(2.6%)
Child Moved Out
of Poor Family

(49.5%)
Earnings of
Head Rose

(10.7%)
Married Couple
Formed

(16.2%)
Other Income Rose

(3.3%)
Earnings of Wife Rose

Author's tabulations from the Panel Study of Income Dynamics.

poverty spells. About 13 percent of poverty spells end with major changes in who heads the family—either a couple gets married, or a child in a poor family leaves and establishes his or her own nonpoor family. Other changes in family composition occur in another 18 percent of cases.

Figure 4 again emphasizes the importance of economic opportunities and the ability of poor adults to find and hold jobs. Most people leave poverty when they or the head of their family receives more earnings. Changes in family composition are less important in escaping poverty than they are in beginning a spell of poverty; for example, a woman and her children are more likely to become poor by leaving a marriage than they are likely to escape poverty by remarrying. From the limited evidence available, marriage is declining in its importance as a way to escape poverty.

Changes in earnings and work opportunities are very important in many families, driving them into poverty or helping them to escape. To a lesser extent, changes in family composition are also important in "creating" and "dissolving" poor families. But the discussion in the first part of this section remains relevant. For some substantial minority among the poor—particularly the black poor—poverty is long-term and escape is infrequent.

THE LACK OF JOB OPPORTUNITIES IN THE INNER CITY

Helene Slessarev

Helene Slessarev discusses the scarcity of jobs in inner-city neighborhoods in the following excerpt from her book *The Betrayal of the Urban Poor*. She explains that in the 1950s and 1960s, more than 3 million blacks left the rural South for industrial cities in the North, drawn by the prospect of better-paying manufacturing jobs. However, she stresses, changes in technology have eliminated most of these jobs, leaving few employment opportunities in inner-city neighborhoods. Racial discrimination has also contributed to the plight of the urban poor, Slessarev argues; for instance, because poor blacks and Latinos live in neighborhoods that are highly segregated, they are cut off from the mainstream labor market. Slessarev contends that it is impossible for the urban poor to lift themselves out of poverty if jobs are not available in the inner-city neighborhoods where they reside.

In 1996, after years of minimal funding for urban anti-poverty efforts, both political parties agreed to withdraw the federal government's sixty-year-old commitment to providing financial support for poor women with children. Remarkably, these changes occurred without either party publicly acknowledging the difficult reality that thirty years after the enactment of basic civil rights reforms, economic opportunities remain as limited as ever for poor minorities living in our nation's cities. As of 1990, 43 percent of the nation's poor were concentrated in America's central cities. Living in neighborhoods that are highly segregated by both race and class, poor African-Americans and Latinos are largely cut off from the society's basic structures of opportunity. Decades of racial segregation have left "the economic base of urban black communities uniquely vulnerable to any downturn in the group's economic fortunes," in the words of Douglas Massey and Nancy Denton. As manufacturing companies left behind their old inner-city facilities during the 1970s and 1980s, segregation quickly triggered a process of neighborhood disinvestment and abandonment. Today, Massey and Denton state, "poor blacks live in communities that typically contain only the rudiments of retail trade." Without an economic base, these communities offer few employment opportunities to the thousands of welfare recipients who will be required to work [as part of the government's welfare reform policy].

Attacking the Poor, Not Poverty

The highly visible growth of urban poverty spawned a virtual cottage industry of academics and policymakers seeking to shed new light on the phenomenon. Conservative writers, who have been the most vocal in their attacks on what they label as liberal welfare policies, have stigmatized poor minorities by arguing that they somehow have "a hidden investment in victimization and poverty," in the words of Shelby Steele. Although these writers correctly identify common attitudes of the poor, their "blame the victim" approach never connects apparent deviant social behavior to the alienation of the poor from the broader society. The conservatives fail to comprehend the link between poverty and powerlessness that leaves poor people constantly having to respond to the actions of others. Life on public aid is the highest expression of such powerlessness because it robs people of the hope of self-advancement through legitimate means. Finding themselves caught between the American myth of equal opportunity and their own inability to achieve their personal dreams, poor people often "internalize their powerlessness as their own fault, rather than as a response to systemwide discrimination," as Nina Wallerstein writes. Much of the deviant behavior displayed by members of the underclass has its roots in their sense of powerlessness. Feeling themselves to be outcasts from mainstream society, they do not see themselves as bound by its norms. Indeed, powerlessness leads to a sense of victimization that can become immobilizing. According to Paulo Freire, "The oppressed, having internalized the image of the oppressor and adopted his guidelines, are fearful of freedom." They become reluctant to believe in the possibility of change, or that they possess the creative capacity to affect their surroundings.

Martin Luther King, Jr., and others involved in the southern civil rights movement understood that their battle for freedom would be won only if large numbers of black people underwent a personal transformation and became conscious of themselves as purposeful actors infused with a sense of dignity and self-worth. Long years of oppression had beaten them down so badly that they doubted their own capacity to improve their conditions. In the South the strategy of nonviolent direct action became the means by which thousands of ordinary blacks divested themselves of their traditional passivity, breaking forever the image of the "shuffling Negro," as King phrased it. Only then could institutional change occur.

Conservatives are oblivious to the continued existence of deep structural barriers that prevent poor minorities from gaining access to the advantages of the dominant society. In *The New Politics of Poverty,* Lawrence Mead simply dismisses poor-quality education, the disappearance of industrial jobs, and the continued presence of racial discrimination, arguing that the existence of powerful social barriers no longer explains why the poor do not work. As he sees it, "motivation is inevitably more at issue than opportunity." Since the social policies of the left and the right have not worked, the fault must lie with the poor themselves. According to Mead, the solutions to poverty lie in the poor becoming "less deviant but more assertive in their own self-interest, especially by working." The often unstated assumption underlying these types of explanations is that all Americans possess equal opportunities for advancement, so that if whole groups of people are falling behind it must be due to their own cultural inadequacies. For example, Nathan Glazer contends that African-Americans have not fared as well because they lack an entrepreneurial spirit and suffer from higher levels of unemployment and social disorganization. Thomas Sowell believes that blacks do not possess the Protestant work ethic required for success. He sees no connection between poor blacks' lack of motivation and their powerlessness, asserting that it is an "arbitrary premise" that the "'disparities' and 'gaps' in incomes and occupations [between whites and blacks] are evidence . . . of discrimination or exploitation."

Closely tied to these cultural arguments are those that place the onus on government social policies, especially those implemented by the Democrats during the 1960s. Supposedly, these anti-poverty efforts were so massive that they made a life of dependency on government aid more attractive than hard work and self-reliance. Charles Murray and George Gilder have both argued that the expanded education, jobs, and welfare programs of the Great Society encouraged laziness and promiscuity and decreased incentive among the urban poor by providing payments to those who chose not to work. According to Murray, "in the late 1960's—at the very moment when the jobs programs began their massive expansion . . . the black youth unemployment rate began to rise again, steeply, and continued to do so throughout the 1970's." The same trends are said to hold for black male labor force participation. Murray blames the liberalization of public aid eligibility for the rise in juvenile delinquency and children born to unwed mothers that occurred in the late 1960s. By making virtually all low-income people welfare recipients, the means-tested programs supposedly robbed them of the social status of working. According to Murray, youths were most affected by this change in the status of work: "In the day to day experience of a youth growing up in a black ghetto there was no evidence whatsoever that working within the system paid off. The way to get something from the system was to be sufficiently a failure to qualify for help, or to con the system."

These authors would have us believe that somehow black inequality was gradually vanishing on its own, rendering any type of government intervention unnecessary. In *Affirmative Discrimination* Glazer presents income and occupational data for the 1950s that show a convergence of black and white incomes, indicating "a virtual collapse in traditional discriminatory patterns in the labor market." Murray goes to considerable lengths in his book *Losing Ground* to prove that during the 1950s and early 1960s black poverty was declining, unemployment was holding steady, and labor force participation rates for blacks were on a par with those of whites from similar backgrounds.

The Loss of Unskilled Jobs

Much of the increase in black income in the 1950s and early 1960s came as the direct result of massive migration out of southern agriculture into industrial employment in the North. Between 1950 and 1970 more than 3 million blacks left the South to replace whites in the industrial labor force, just as new technologies were being introduced that would soon eliminate many of the unskilled jobs on the assembly line. In fact, 1953 was the last year of relatively low black unemployment, 4.4 percent for males and 3.7 percent for females. By 1962, the rates were 10 percent and 9.8 percent, respectively, more than twice the unemployment level among whites, while for black teenagers it was already a shocking 23.6 percent. Those occupations in which unemployment was the highest—for example, laborers, operatives, and "other service workers"—were precisely the occupations in which blacks were most concentrated. Conversely, the occupations with the lowest unemployment rates, such as managers, officials, and proprietors, were those in which blacks were least concentrated. The move from agriculture to industrial labor did not bring the majority of blacks any closer to the center of American economic life. By the end of 1963, at least 750,000 black youth were roaming the streets, out of school and out of work.

It does not take a great deal of complex social science research to conclude that today there are few jobs left in poor minority communities. A drive through streets lined with boarded-up factories, warehouses, and stores will suffice. It has been estimated that between 30 and 50 percent of the employment gap between white and black youth can be explained by differences in job accessibility. A recent labor market study in Illinois found that there are four potential entry-level job seekers for every entry-level job available in the state. In Chicago the ratio was even higher—six job seekers for every available entry-level job. The loss of manufacturing jobs and the high concentration of poorly trained African-Americans and Hispanics has placed the demographics and economics of America's cities on a collision course. Although the overall educational attainment of urban minorities improved during the 1970s and 1980s, these gains were not sufficient to keep pace with even faster rises in the education required to work in the new urban information-based economy. Yet, conservatives would have us think that jobs are plentiful. For example, Mead contends that "since the 1960s, opportunities have grown for the low-skilled. Their education levels as well as the number of jobs have risen. Racial discrimination has fallen, as have welfare disincentives, with the failure of AFDC [Aid to Families with Dependent Children] benefits, since the early 1970's, to keep pace with inflation." The decline in factory jobs was supposedly offset by "an explosion of employment in service trades." Thus, Mead concludes, "Most inner-city poor appear able to find jobs, albeit not of the quality they would like."

Creating Economic Opportunity

A true pledge to alleviate poverty would require a commitment to building structures of economic opportunity. Every economy has such structures, both formal and informal, designed to move each successive generation to a new level of economic security. In poor minority communities, these structures are often nonexistent or in acute disrepair, leaving the majority of residents without any real possibility of economic advancement. Given America's legacy of racial oppression, establishing structures of economic opportunity for people of color would entail more than just competent schools, career training, available employment, childcare, and job referrals. It would require opening up the entire metropolitan labor market, which is now so geographically and occupationally stratified by race and class that poor minorities are confined to only a tiny fraction of the total job opportunities. It would include a commitment to eliminating all remaining forms of racial exclusion, even though they are not legally sanctioned. The lack of access to the mainstream labor market lies at the heart of the urban crisis of poverty. The departure of low-skill manufacturing jobs, continued employment discrimination, and the poor quality of urban education work together to condemn large segments of black and Latino communities to a marginal economic status.

SINGLE-PARENT FAMILIES ARE MORE LIKELY TO BE POOR

Patrick F. Fagan

According to Patrick F. Fagan, the likelihood of whether a child will live in poverty is greatly influenced by the marital status of the child's parents. Studies show that children of single parents are six times more likely to be impoverished than children whose parents are married, Fagan asserts. In fact, he notes, divorce is closely linked to poverty: Almost half of all families that are broken by divorce become impoverished. Children born out of wedlock, especially to teenage mothers, also experience high rates of poverty, the author explains. This cycle often continues in the next generation, Fagan maintains, since children of single parents are more likely to get pregnant before marriage, which lessens the likelihood that they will complete their education and obtain a good-paying job—thus making it more likely that their children will also be raised in poverty. Fagan is the William H.G. FitzGerald Senior Fellow in family and cultural issues at the Heritage Foundation.

Much of the debate about the growing gap between rich and poor in America focuses on the changing job force, the cost of living, and the tax and regulatory structure that hamstrings businesses and employees. But analysis of the social science literature demonstrates that the root cause of poverty and income disparity is linked undeniably to the presence or absence of marriage. Broken families earn less and experience lower levels of educational achievement. Worse, they pass the prospect of meager incomes and family instability on to their children, ensuring a continuing if not expanding cycle of economic distress.

Marriage Has a Massive Effect

Simply put, whether or not a child's parents are married and stay married has a massive effect on his or her future prosperity and that of the next generation. Unfortunately, the growth in the number of children born into broken families in America—from 12 for every 100

From "How Broken Families Rob Children of Their Chances for Future Prosperity," by Patrick F. Fagan, *Heritage Foundation Backgrounder*, June 11, 1999. Copyright © 1999 by The Heritage Foundation. Reprinted with permission.

born in 1950 to 58 for every 100 born in 1992—has become a seemingly unbreakable cycle that the federal government not only continues to ignore, but even promotes through some of its policies.

Numerous academic and social science researchers have demonstrated how the path to achieving a decent and stable income is still the traditional one: complete school, get a job, get married, then have children, in that order. Obviously, the journey toward a secure income can be derailed by choices growing children make, such as dropping out of school or getting pregnant before marriage. But generally, children who grow up in a stable, two-parent family have the best prospects for achieving income security as adults.

Because of recent advances in the methods social scientists and economists use to collect data, researchers are taking a broader intergenerational view of America's poor. From this vantage point, it has become clear that federal policies over the past three decades have promoted welfare dependency and single-parent families over married parents while frittering away the benefits of a vigorous free market and strong economy. Today, the economic and social future of children in the poor and the middle class is being undermined by a culture that promotes teenage sex, divorce, cohabitation, and out-of-wedlock birth.

Fortunately, the federal government and states and local communities can play important roles in changing this culture to ensure that all children reach their full income potential and do not languish in the poverty trap.

The Link Between Divorce and Poverty

To understand the importance of marriage to prosperity, and what the determinants of a stable marriage are, it is important to look first at the evidence surrounding the effects of its alternatives—divorce, cohabitation, and out-of-wedlock births—on children and on income.

Sadly, almost half of American families experience poverty following a divorce, and 75 percent of all women who apply for welfare benefits do so because of a disrupted marriage or a disrupted relationship in which they live with a male outside of marriage.

Divorce has many harmful effects on the income of families and future generations. Its immediate effects can be seen in data reported in 1994 by Mary Corcoran, a professor of political science at the University of Michigan: "During the years children lived with two parents, their family incomes averaged $43,600, and when these same children lived with one parent, their family incomes averaged $25,300." In other words, the household income of a child's family dropped on average about 42 percent following divorce. By 1997, 8.15 million children were living with a divorced single parent. There has been an increase of 354 percent since 1950.

As substantial as this income reduction is, little public attention is paid to the relationship between the breakdown of marriage and poverty. Consider, by comparison, the reaction to a comparable decrease in the national economy. When America's economic productivity fell by 2.1 percent from 1981 to 1982, it was called a recession. And when the economy contracted by 30.5 percent from $203 million to $141 million (in constant 1958 dollars) from 1929 to 1933, it was called the Great Depression. Yet each and every year for the past 27 years, over one million children have experienced divorce in their families with an associated reduction in family income that ranged from 28 percent to 42 percent. It is no wonder that three-fourths of all women applying for welfare benefits do so because of a disruption of marriage.

Understandably, mothers who are employed at the time of divorce are much less likely to become welfare recipients than are mothers who do not work. And mothers who are not employed in the workforce at the time of divorce are as close to going on welfare as are single mothers who lose their jobs. Divorce is the main factor in determining the length of "poverty spells," particularly for women whose pre-divorce family income was in the bottom half of the income distribution. Divorce, then, poses the greatest threat to women in low-income families. Moreover, almost 50 percent of households with children move into poverty following divorce. Simply put, divorce has become too prevalent and affects an ever-increasing number of children.

In the 1950s, the rate of divorce was lower among high-income groups; by 1960, there was a convergence of rates among all socioeconomic groups. By 1975, for the first time, more marriages ended in divorce than in death. Since 1960, there has been a significant shift in the ratio of children deprived of married parents by death compared with those so deprived by divorce. Compared with the number of children who lost a parent through death, 75 percent, 150 percent, and 580 percent as many, respectively, lost a parent through divorce in 1960, in 1986, and in 1995.

The Problems Caused by Divorce

Divorce is linked to a number of serious problems beyond the immediate economic problem of lost income. For instance, the children of divorced parents are more likely to get pregnant and give birth outside of marriage, especially if the divorce occurred during their mid-teenage years, and twice as likely to cohabit than are children of married parents. Moreover, divorce appears to result in a reduction of the educational accomplishments of the affected children, weakens their psychological and physical health, and predisposes them to rapid initiation of sexual relationships and higher levels of marital instability. It also raises the probability that they will never marry, especially for boys.

For a mother with children, divorce increases her financial responsibility and, typically, her hours of labor outside the home. Divorce and additional work hours also disrupt her network of support for parenting her children. These additional stresses take their toll: Single mothers experience increased levels of physical and mental illness, addictions, and even suicide following divorce. All of these outcomes have an effect on family income.

Moreover, the consequences of divorce flow from generation to generation, since the children of divorce are more likely to experience the same problems and pass them on to their own children. Significantly, these effects are markedly different from the effect that the death of a married parent has on children; in fact, such children are *less* likely than the average to divorce when they grow up.

Divorce and Asset Formation

Little research has been done on the effect of divorce on the assets accumulated over time by a household, but a RAND Corporation study indicates that the effect may be dramatic: Family structure is strongly tied to wealth by the time one reaches the sixth decade of life. The assets of married couples in their fifties (who are approaching retirement) are four times greater than those of their divorced peers. Even when the two divorced households' assets on average are combined, the RAND study shows that their asset base is half that of married couples.

Upon reflection, this makes sense. After a divorce, the largest asset—the family home—frequently is sold and the proceeds used to finance the divorce and start new homes. In addition, the evidence indicates that the income of divorced households with children drops significantly, thereby lessening the likelihood of asset formation. . . .

Out-of-Wedlock Births and Poverty

Today, social science research broadly characterizes the children who are most likely to attain a good income as adults: They have parents who are married; they finish school, get a job, abstain from intercourse until marriage, and marry before having children of their own. But family structure plays an even larger role in children's future prosperity than those who have formulated public policy over the past 30 years have been willing to admit.

Having a baby out of wedlock usually derails progress toward achieving a stable family structure and income. Teenage out-of-wedlock births rose from 15 percent of all teen births in 1960 to 76 percent in 1994. Fewer than one-third of those who have a baby before reaching age 18 complete high school, compared with the 50 percent completion rate for teens of similar backgrounds who avoid pregnancy.

It is not that the number of babies born to teens has changed; it is that marriage within this group has vanished. In addition, almost half of the mothers of out-of-wedlock children will go on to have another child out of wedlock.

Chart 1. Median Income of Families with Children by Structure

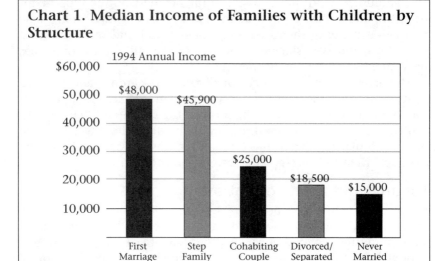

Note: Figures do not include transferred income.

Heritage Center for Data Analysis calculations based on data from *1995 Survey of Consumer Finance*, Federal Reserve Board.

The vast majority of out-of-wedlock births occur to mature adults age 20 and older, and more out-of-wedlock births occur to women over 30 than to teens below age 18; the number is eight times higher for second out-of-wedlock births. The increase in these births among older women accompanies a decline in teenage out-of-wedlock births and abortions.

Two very different changes in American society may explain this decline: the rise in teenage virginity and an increase in the use of contraceptives. The editor of *Teen People* magazine recently reported very high interest among teenagers in the subject of virginity. Access to the specific implant contraceptives Depro-Provera and Norplant also has been associated (but not documented as yet) with the reduction in the number of out-of-wedlock teen births. Aside from the avoidance of pregnancy, the decision not to abstain from sex is linked to habits of risk-taking related to alcohol and drug abuse, school dropout rates, and crime.

The Risk of Poverty Among Single Parents

More than any other group, teenage mothers who give birth outside of marriage spend more of their lives as single parents. Not surprisingly, their children spend more time in poverty than do the children of any other family structure.

A single-parent family background and the poverty that usually accompanies it render children twice as likely to drop out of high school, 2.5 times as likely to become out-of-wedlock teen parents, and 1.4 times as likely to be unemployed. These teens miss more days of school, have lower educational aspirations, receive lower grades, and eventually divorce more often as adults. They are almost twice as likely to exhibit antisocial behavior as adults; 25 percent to 50 percent more likely to manifest such behavioral problems as anxiety, depression, hyperactivity, or dependence; two to three times more likely to need psychiatric care; and much more likely to commit suicide as teenagers.

Mark Testa, a professor in the University of Chicago's School of Social Service Administration, conducted studies that show the linkage between family background, education, and work habits and out-of-wedlock pregnancy. According to Testa, "premarital pregnancy risks are significantly higher among single women who are not in school or [are] out of work and who have dropped out of high school. Being raised in a family that received welfare also appears to raise the risk of premarital pregnancy."

The Downward Spiral

The research of Yuko Matsuhashi of the University of California at San Diego and his colleagues shows that few mothers (14 percent) were living with both parents at the time of their first out-of-wedlock baby's conception, and fewer still (2 percent) were living with both parents at the time of their second baby's conception. In other words, single-parent households become much more entrenched with the

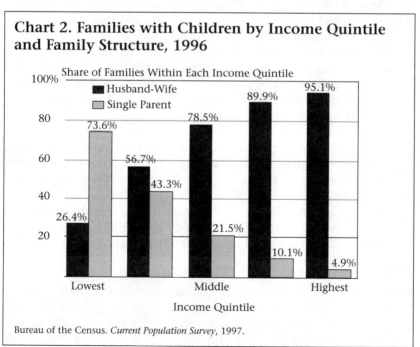

Chart 2. Families with Children by Income Quintile and Family Structure, 1996

Bureau of the Census. *Current Population Survey*, 1997.

second baby, and fewer of these mothers stay in school, thereby lessening their chances of attaining a good income in the future.

Nearly 80 percent of men do not marry the teenage mothers of their children. Nonetheless, cohabitation and cooperation in some form generally does occur between biological parents. About 40 percent of mothers plan to care for their first baby with the father of the baby, but not to marry him. Many more mothers of second out-of-wedlock babies plan to take care of their babies alone than do the mothers of first out-of-wedlock babies, and fewer of them live with their own parents. The downward economic spiral accelerates.

Typically, the household income of those who have out-of-wedlock children in their teens is low. Over 75 percent will be on welfare within five years. These women comprise more than half of all mothers on welfare. The average family income for children who lived with their never-married mothers was only about 40 percent of the family income for children who lived with either a divorced or a widowed mother. The family background of most teenage out-of-wedlock mothers includes such factors as early age at marriage (or cohabitation) for the teen mother's own parents and lower educational levels for both the teen mother's parents and the teen mother herself.

The Family Structure of Child Poverty

As Chart 1 shows, the relationship between poverty and the absence of intact marriages is indeed very strong. The continuous cooperation and lifelong commitment involved in marriage have much to do with significant income differences in households with children. For example:

- *The vast majority of children who live with a single parent are in households in the bottom 20 percent of earnings.* Specifically, about 74 percent of families with children in the lowest income quintile are headed by single parents. Conversely, 95 percent of families with children in the highest quintile of income are headed by married parents. (See Chart 2.)
- *Children living with a single mother are six times more likely to live in poverty than are children whose parents are married.* As this analysis will show, family background also can be linked with less education and fewer hours worked, on average, when the child grows up.
- *Over 12.5 million children in 1994 lived in single-parent families that earned less than $15,000 per year.* Only 3 million such children lived with families that had annual incomes greater than $30,000.

Why Family Structure Affects Income

The research discussed above clearly indicates that family structure has much to do with income levels and asset building, both of which lead to economic prosperity. This section will explain why this occurs.

A family's income is used to finance immediate needs and, if it is sufficient, may allow the family to save for future needs. There are two elements in the amount of income received: the dollar value of hours worked and the number of hours worked. These in turn are affected by, among other things, the parents' education level and work habits that typically are formed in the early years.

The marriage of the parents has much to do with a child's educational attainment and work ethic. The relationship can be expressed as an equation: Income = (education attained) x (work ethic) x (unity of family structure).

Marriage, Education, and Income

Of course, one does not obtain an adequate and steady income just by marrying. Increasing the number of hours worked at a job valued by the marketplace will provide more income. The number of hours worked is linked directly to educational achievement and family structure. Families whose members have lower levels of education normally will have to work longer to reach a modest level of financial security than do those whose members achieve higher levels of education.

However, people who are not married and have less education work the fewest hours per year. In general, married couples have higher levels of education and work longer, and make sure that their children achieve higher levels of education.

Although the income of a family household depends on the educational level of parents, it is the parents' *income* rather than their *level of education* that predicts more accurately the level of education their children will achieve. In general, children with high-income parents receive more education than do children of lower-income parents. But higher income is less likely without marriage (see Chart 1), and poverty is much more likely without it.

Education gives the child from a high-income family a great advantage. The federal government's Panel Study of Income Dynamics showed the large economic gains that can be realized by completing high school, both in the level of wages earned and in the longer hours per week that a person will work. But family background accounts for at least half the variance in educational attainment. Students from intact families score more positively on all measures than do those from both step and single-parent families. Adolescents who do not live with both natural parents are at significantly greater risk of leaving high school before graduating. And the number of years of education received translates into a better first job and better jobs later at higher salaries.

Marriage, Work Ethic, and Income

A significant portion of two-parent families have moved out of the poverty range because both parents work, which also increases—and in many cases doubles—the total number of hours worked within the household. Among America's poor, there has been a significant shift in the number of hours worked per household, which indicates that much of the disparity in young men's economic status is concentrated in the number of hours worked.

In 1960, nearly two-thirds of households in the bottom quintile of income were headed by individuals who worked—primarily married fathers. By 1991, this figure had fallen to around one-third, and only 11 percent of these households were headed by someone who worked full-time throughout the year.

The total number of hours worked in married households has increased significantly over the past 40 years. According to former Congressional Budget Office Director June O'Neill, in 1950 only 18 percent of married mothers with children under 18 worked outside the home. By 1975, 41 percent of married mothers worked and that proportion reached 64 percent in 1992. Yet mothers on welfare appear to work little—only 7 percent report any employment. (These data were collected before the enforcement of the Welfare Reform Act (1996).)

Not only are those in the lowest quintile generally working fewer hours than their counterparts were in the 1950s and 1960s, but they are doing so despite a national family trend in the rising number of hours worked.

A reverse trend accompanies the disappearance of marriage: The number of hours worked in the family household declines. Present-day single heads of households are working fewer hours than the married heads of poor households in the 1950s (typically, married men). At the same time, married couples are increasing the total number of hours worked, and although there are some unwelcome consequences from this increase in working hours in married households, there is no doubt that it has increased the number of families exiting a life of poverty.

Welfare's Impact on the Number of Hours Worked

Welfare payments have had a predictable if pernicious effect on the overall response of recipients to marriage as well as work. Consider data from the past decade. Again, according to former CBO Director June O'Neill:

> Findings from the Seattle–Denver Income Maintenance Experiment (U.S. Office of Income Security Policy, 1983) show that female heads of families responded to income guarantees by significantly reducing their work effort. Other studies have found that women are less likely to work in states with high levels of AFDC [Aid to Families with Dependent Children] benefits.

Historically, O'Neill found, higher welfare benefit levels have had dramatic negative effects on the behavior of young men, especially young African-American males, by reducing their participation in the workforce and increasing the likelihood that they will father a child or children out of wedlock. Sheldon Danziger, professor at the School of Social Policy at the University of Michigan, concluded in 1986 that because only one-third of the poor were expected to work, most poor households would not benefit from an improved economy. Thus, even when the national economy improved, welfare families who were disconnected from a market-based economy remained stuck in poverty because their income was not connected to the number of hours worked or to a rise in the hourly value of their labor that is commonly connected with a more robust economy.

The Value of Effort

If the level of education and the number of hours worked are important to a child's future income, the acquisition of a positive work ethic is vital. If a child's parents already espouse a belief in effort, the child has a much better chance of believing in the positive results of effort.

For some time, social scientists have presented "personal effort believers" as typically successful, competent, and emotionally stable people. Their opposites are "external pressure believers," who tend not to make long-term plans or to think of ways to control or change their circumstances since they do not believe their efforts will really matter. The latter group generally is far less successful.

Martin Seligman, professor of psychology at the University of Pennsylvania and president of the American Psychological Association, is world-renowned for his work on changing external pressure believers into personal effort believers and on learned optimism and learned helplessness. His work on "Learned Efficacy/Learned Optimism" shows that the coaching children receive from their parents and teachers as they tackle the early and tougher tasks of life has everything to do with deep-seated beliefs they acquire regarding effort (beyond their own awareness).

Learned helplessness also can be acquired in the early years, with such beliefs frequently having taken hold by age six. Many of the children who are external pressure believers jeopardize their economic future in adolescence by dropping out of school or getting pregnant before marriage.

The presence or absence of a belief in effort, then, has much to do with poverty or attaining a desired income level. Middle-class children are more likely to pick up belief in effort from their parents and teachers. Children raised on welfare, in many cases, have the opposite experience. The longer a person is on welfare, the greater the erosion of the belief in effort. Some welfare recipients report that they are aware of the bad effects welfare has on attitudes within their families, but having a low belief in their own abilities, they see few viable alternatives. In other words, they lose confidence.

As the research cited above shows, parents' achievement in the

marketplace leads to achievement by their children in the school-
room. The earlier the parents pass on a belief in effort, the longer and
deeper the educational and economic benefits to the child will be. . . .

The Importance of Marriage

Marital and family stability is undeniably linked to economic prosperity for American families. Even though America has achieved a level
of prosperity unrivaled in history, too many families still do not share
in these benefits. The effects of marital breakdown on national prosperity and the well-being of individual children are like the action of
termites on the beams in a home's foundation: They are weakening,
quietly but seriously, the structural underpinnings of society.

The contradiction between Washington's concern for economic
prosperity and its disregard for stable marriage and family life must be
resolved. The longer reform is delayed, the more children will be
doomed to living in poverty with its life-changing effects. Congress,
state legislators, community leaders, and church officials can and must
take clear steps to restore the primacy of marriage—the backbone of
the family and society in America.

IMMIGRATION IS RESPONSIBLE FOR THE RISING POVERTY RATE

Linda Thom

Millions of uneducated and poor Hispanics and Asians immigrate to the United States every year, Linda Thom writes in the following selection, and these immigrants are contributing to the U.S. poverty rate. She explains that between 1989 and 1997, the U.S. poverty rate increased by 4 million people, more than 3 million of whom were Hispanic or Asian immigrants. During the same time period, according to Thom, the poverty rate for blacks and non-Hispanic whites decreased. In fact, she contends, the U.S. poverty rate would be declining were it not for the influx of impoverished Hispanic and Asian immigrants. In addition, she notes, child poverty rates—which are declining among blacks and non-Hispanic whites—are on the increase among Hispanics and Asians. Thom concludes that the explosion in the Hispanic child poverty rate is accounted for in part by poor immigrants, whose birthrate is twice as high as that of native-born women. Thom is a retired budget analyst for the Santa Barbara, California, County Administrator's Office.

On September 24, 1998, the United States Census Bureau issued two press releases to accompany their annual report on poverty, *Poverty in the United States: 1997*. The release headlines read: *Poverty Rate Down, Household Income up—Both Return to 1989 Pre-Recession Levels* and *Poverty Level of Hispanic Population Drops, Income Improves.*

What impression do these headlines give? Most would probably read them and believe that after years of grim economic times, Americans are again thriving and that Hispanics, especially, are making good economic progress. Unfortunately, the headlines are partially true at best and disingenuous at worst.

What the Bureau Did Not Say

What the Bureau *did not say* is that the number of poor people increased by 4 million between 1989 and 1997 even if, according to

From "America's Immigrant-Driven Poverty Increase," by Linda Thom, *Social Contract*, Winter 1998–1999. Copyright © 1999 by Linda Thom. Reprinted by permission of *Social Contract*.

Dr. Daniel Weinberg who led the press briefing, "the poverty rate is statistically no different from the pre-recession rate in 1989." (Actually, the poverty rate is not down as the headline says but rather up from 12.8 percent in 1989 to 13.3 percent in 1997, but this information is buried in the full one-hundred-page poverty report in one of the probably 50 pages of tables). Further, the Bureau *did say* that the drop in Hispanic poverty rates "accounted for a significant share of the decrease in the overall poverty rate between 1996 and 1997." That is what happened in one year. What the Bureau *did not say* is that the Hispanic poor accounted for almost three quarters of the 4 million increase in America's poor since 1989.

If the data for the period are disaggregated by race and ethnicity, Hispanics and Asians accounted for 84 percent of the added poor people since 1989. Blacks in poverty declined by 186,000 and "others" in poverty increased by 825,000. Others are mostly non-Hispanic whites and Native Americans. While it is true that table upon table of data are available in the Census Bureau's document, *Poverty in the United States: 1997*, who knows anyone in the media who sits down and analyses the data to see what press releases have left unsaid. The media take the press summaries prepared for them, listen to the briefing, and that is what goes to press. Unfortunately, the Census Bureau did not disaggregate the data and, by leaving so much unsaid, left the impression that all is well in America.

The Bureau's failure to publicly announce that there has been a huge increase in poor people since 1989 and that Hispanics and Asians caused most of that increase continues to keep the truth from the American people and from American policy makers. The truth is that both the numbers living in poverty and the poverty rate would be declining in America were it not for immigration—and that, despite a booming economy, many immigrants are dying on the vine.

The Real Story

The press releases cited above accompanied the release of the Bureau's annual report on poverty, *Poverty in the United States: 1997*. Buried in the body of the report itself, the Bureau does indicate that in 1997, the poverty rate for both native-born Americans and foreign-born residents declined and now stands at 12.5 percent for the native-born as compared to 19.9 percent for foreign-born residents. The Bureau's report also notes, ". . . the foreign-born population was disproportionately poor when compared with natives of the United States." Nowhere, however, does the report indicate that it is manifestly clear that in the last decade, virtually all the added poor people are Hispanics and Asians and that may have something to do with immigration.

In addition to poverty rates by nativity, the Bureau provides poverty rates by race and ethnicity. The Bureau's press conferences and press releases state the current poverty rates and changes from the prior year. The one year poverty rates are in the right direction—down. This peek at the numbers reveals little and focusing only on the changes in the poverty rate is downright misleading if the numbers of poor people are increasing.

The federal government defines poverty thresholds by income and number of family members. In 1997, the poverty threshold for a family of four was an income of $16,400 a year. In 1989, the income threshold for a family of four was $12,674. In 1997, 35.6 million people were poor, up by over 4 million from 31.5 million in 1989. Despite this increase of 4 million poor people, the 1997 poverty rate was up only slightly from 1989. The poverty rate is calculated by dividing the number of poor people by the entire population. Thus, 35,574,000 poor divided by 268,480,000 people results in an overall poverty rate of 13.3 percent in 1997.

In 1989, 12.8 percent of America's 246 million residents were poor and in 1997, 13.3 percent of the 268 million people were poor. The Census Bureau correctly states that an increase in the poverty rate of half a percent is not statistically significant. What is statistically significant, however, is that poor people increased by 4 million. The nation has a growing poverty problem, not one which is statistically unchanged. The population increased by 22 million and of those added people, 4 million were poor. So what if the poverty rate in 1997 is not statistically different from the pre-recession 1989 rate? This is a losing proposition.

Table One shows the changes in poor people by race and ethnicity from 1989 to 1997. The category "others" is almost entirely non-Hispanic whites but also includes Native Americans and others.

Table One: Change in Numbers of Poor People by Race and Ethnicity, 1989 to 1997

(Numbers Are in Thousands)

YEAR	All Poor	Asian	Black	Hispanic	Others
1997	35,574	1,468	9,116	8,308	16,682
1989	31,528	939	9,302	5,430	15,857
Change 1989–97	4,046	529	–186	2,878	825
Percent of Total Change	100%	13%	Decline	71%	20%
1997 Poverty Rate	13.3%	14.0%	26.5%	27.1%	8.6%
1989 Poverty Rate	12.8%	14.1%	30.7%	26.2%	8%

The number of poor people increased by 4 million but observe that, together, the number of Hispanic and Asian poor people rose by 3.4 million. Even though poor Hispanic people increased by 2.9 million, their poverty rate only rose by nine-tenths of a percent. The Asian poverty rate declined by one-tenth of a percent but there are 529,000 more Asian poor people. Focusing on poverty rate and not numbers in poverty is completely misleading.

Actually the picture is worse than the numbers suggest. Some might believe that an increasing population will always increase the number of poor people, but that is incorrect. Table Two shows the change in population by race and ethnicity from pre-recession 1989 to 1997. Tables One and Two show that the black population increased by 4.1 million but the black poor decreased by 186,000 between 1989 and 1997. Some might counter that the population of Hispanics and Asians is growing rapidly and, therefore, the number of poor increased rapidly. That is true—Hispanics and Asians accounted for 61 percent of the population growth between 1989 and 1997 but they accounted for 84 percent of the poverty increase. Others accounted for 21 percent of the population growth but only 8 percent of the growth in poor people. Poverty among Hispanics and Asians is growing faster than their share of population growth. Blacks are making tremendous strides, especially in the last few years and others' numbers are growing but those in poverty are growing much more slowly.

Between 1989 and 1997, Asians accounted for 17 percent of the total U.S. population increase but accounted for 13 percent of all the added poor people. The absolute number of added poor Asians increased by 56 percent and their total population grew by 57 percent. This does not seem so bad unless it is compared to the tremendous progress of blacks. If blacks can make such great strides in the current economy, then why is it that many Asians cannot?

Black people have a very high poverty rate—26.5 percent in 1997 compared to the Asian poverty rate of 14 percent. But the black

Table Two: Change in Population by Race and Ethnicity, 1989 to 1997

(Numbers Are in Thousands)

YEAR	All	Asian	Black	Hispanic	Others
1997	268,480	10,482	24,458	30,637	192,903
1989	245,992	6,673	30,332	20,746	188,241
Change 1989–97	22,488	3,809	4,126	9,891	4,662
% of Total Change	100%	17%	18%	44%	21%

Table Three: 1997 Child Poverty Rates by Race and Ethnicity				
All Children	Asian	Black	Hispanic	Others
19.9%	20.3%	37.2%	36.8%	11.5%

poverty rate declined from 30.7 percent in 1989 to 26.5 percent currently and for the last several years has been lower than the Hispanic poverty rate which was 27.1 percent in 1997. This turn around for black Americans contrasts to the sobering escalation of poor Hispanics and Asians.

The plight of Hispanics and Asians is abysmal but for children it is worse. In 1997, the poverty rate for Asian and Hispanic children was increasing, not decreasing, while the rates for whites and blacks are declining. Overall, the number of poor children in America increased by 1.5 million and Asian and Hispanic children accounted for all of the increase and then some because their poor increased by 1.6 million. Not only did the number of poor black children decline by 150,000, their poverty rate declined from 43.7 percent to 37.2 percent. These numbers are still distressingly high, but they are headed in the right direction because the number of black children increased by 1.7 million even as their numbers in poverty declined. Table Three displays 1997 child poverty rates by race and ethnicity.

The Immigration Connection

Are the increases in Asian and Hispanic poverty connected to immigration? Of course they are. Currently, three quarters of new arrivals on America's shores are Hispanic or Asian. In 1990, two of every three Asians living in the United States were foreign-born and among Hispanics two of every three were foreign-born or the children of immigrants.

But the increase results not just from immigrants moving to America but also to the increase in United States–citizen children born to immigrants. Between 1989 and 1996, data from the United States Department of Health and Human Services show that births to native-born women are decreasing just as births to immigrants are increasing. Moreover, not only the number but the percent of all births is shifting. In 1989, 85.2 percent of America's 3.9 million births were to native-born mothers. By 1996, the percentage had dropped to 80.8 percent of the 3.9 million births. Between 1989 and 1996, Hispanic women, native and immigrant, gave birth to 5.1 million babies and Asians gave birth to 1 million children. In 1996, 62 percent of Hispanic new mothers were immigrants and 85 percent of Asian new mothers were immigrants.

Of the 701,339 Hispanic births in 1996, 70 percent were to Mexican-origin women who were both native and foreign-born. Unfortunately, this large subgroup of Hispanics has a very high fertility rate and it is rising. In 1989, Mexican-origin women had a fertility rate of 94.5 births per 1,000 population of women in childbearing years and by 1996, the rate jumped to 120.7 per 1,000. This compares to the fertility of non-Hispanic black women which dropped from 84.8 per 1,000 in 1989 to 72.5 per 1,000 in 1996 and non-Hispanic white women whose rate dropped from 60.5 to 57.3. The range of rates was not available for Asian women but the rate in 1996 was 65.9 per 1000 women of childbearing age. Note the 1996 Mexican-origin fertility rate of 120.7 in comparison to the black rate of 72.5, the white rate of 57.3 and the Asian rate of 65.9. Clearly, both immigration and the high Mexican-origin fertility rate is driving the explosion in the Hispanic child population and the Hispanic child poverty growth.

Immigration Is Responsible

Because so many immigrants are Hispanic and Asian and because so many Hispanic and Asian new mothers are foreign-born, the conclusion is obvious: immigration is driving most of the increase in population and in poverty. But the numbers in poverty are increasing faster than the rise in population. Even so, why does America need any more poor people? And why is the Census Bureau failing to give the bad news? More important, why is the Bureau slanting its releases to the press by saying that all is well? The recession is over and everybody is doing fine; that is the impression the press is given and then the press releases this distortion to the American people. The press cannot be blamed for this. News writers do words, not numbers. The Census Bureau does numbers and as the government agency in charge of the numbers, the Bureau is accountable for providing complete and accurate information. The truths are:

- America is importing millions and millions of uneducated, poor people with high fertility rates.
- The Census Bureau is not disclosing the facts.
- The American people and American policy makers will never know the facts unless the Census Bureau starts disclosing the real story and not misleading America about immigration's impact on poverty.

The really disturbing part of this is that even if the United States significantly curtails immigration and changes to a skills-based legal immigration policy, the huge base of poorly educated immigrants with high fertility rates will continue to plague America for years to come. Those who are less pessimistic should consider that more than one hundred thirty years have passed since America freed black slaves. Today, blacks still struggle to achieve the American dream and the country still continues to wrestle with the consequences of this prior wave of cheap, foreign labor.

CHAPTER 3

SOLVING THE PROBLEM OF INNER-CITY POVERTY

A "Living Wage" Is Necessary to Help the Working Poor

Neal Peirce

People who work at minimum-wage jobs are often unable to make ends meet, notes syndicated columnist Neal Peirce in the following article. In many cities where the cost of living is high, he explains, these workers would have to earn two to four times the minimum wage just to be able to afford the average rent of a modest apartment. Peirce contends that these expensive cities could help the working poor by establishing a "living wage," which is the salary they would need—usually well above the federally mandated minimum wage—to enable them to meet their basic living expenses in the communities where they work. According to the author, many cities have already instituted living wage laws that require companies that do business with local governments to pay their workers adequately.

The working poor. They're critical to the American Economic Machine. Whether they're janitors or maids, store clerks or hamburger tossers at fast food outlets, airport baggage screeners or hospital workers, we count on them all.

And there's good news: Some are doing better. A Census report indicates America's phenomenally durable economic expansion is touching more and more people. The poverty rate is down to 11.8 percent, or 32 million people, the lowest percentage since 1979. Gains are especially dramatic for blacks and Hispanic-Americans.

But there's a "cruel irony," notes [former] Housing and Urban Development Secretary Andrew Cuomo: While the economy delivers prosperity for millions, it's also driving up rents. The number of households with worst-case housing needs—living in clearly substandard housing, and/or paying more than 50 percent of their income for housing—has expanded to a record 5.4 million households.

Inadequate Housing

Across America, millions of working families, folks who failed to cash in on stock market expansion or the new global economy, are forced to double up in seedy, overcrowded apartments. Whole families share single bedrooms. Some sleep in their cars. Many full-time workers have to choose between paying the rent or paying for food, medical care or child care.

There's not a single county in the United States where a worker earning the federal minimum wage ($5.15 an hour in 2000) can afford a "modest" two-bedroom apartment by federal standards.

The National Low Income Housing Coalition calculates a "fair market rent"—the income a family needs to pay no more than 30 percent of its pretax earnings for housing. The national average fair market rent for 1999 was $12.47 an hour—more than *twice* the federal minimum wage.

And in some hot-growth areas, the situation is even worse. In California's Marin, San Francisco and San Mateo Counties, a worker would need to earn $28.06 an hour for an average apartment. In Santa Clara County (Silicon Valley) it's $25.12. In the city of Los Angeles, teeming with 4 million people (a third of them immigrants) and home to some of America's most dramatic income disparities, the hourly pay would have to be $17. Low wages and high rents, notes Peter Dreier of Occidental College, make for "a deadly combination."

In more than half of America's metro areas, fair market rent is at least twice the minimum wage. And U.S. child poverty remains higher than that of most advanced nations.

Can we claim a just American society when we tolerate these frightening disparities? Are we sowing a whirlwind of future bitterness, divisiveness? As the AFL-CIO notes, if a minimum-wage worker's pay had grown as fast in the past five years as pay of CEOs of American corporations, it would now be $49,000—$23 an hour.

And the issue is bigger than justice. Wages high enough to afford safe and decent housing, Cuomo notes, "are the key to family well-being, educational success, and productive work." The whole society, in other words, benefits.

Yet the Republican congressional majority, pushed by small-business interests, won't tolerate even a minor minimum-wage increase.

A Living Wage

There is real hope at the local level, where there's a strong "living wage" movement to require that any company that gets subsidies or significant contracts from local government pay its workers a wage well above the federal minimum—often the salary a worker needs to get above the poverty line.

A coalition of labor and religious officials got Baltimore to pass the first of these laws in 1994. Since then some 50 cities have followed, among them St. Louis, Boston, Los Angeles, San Jose, Portland, Milwaukee, Detroit, Minneapolis and Miami-Dade County.

Living wage's strongest national advocate has been the Association of Community Organizations for Reform Now (ACORN), an advocate for low-income people with 100,000 members in some 30 cities. Right now ACORN is giving a hand to 75 living wage campaigns, including efforts in Philadelphia, New Orleans, Dallas, Sacramento and Washington, D.C.

In Santa Monica, Calif., community activists argue the local tourism industry has received huge public investments and it's time to guarantee wages of at least $10.69 an hour to hotel, restaurant and store workers in the trendy town's booming "coastal zone." Business interests, trying to forestall that, are pushing a ballot measure that would actually help just 200 workers.

There is, in fact, a hollow ring to business arguments that living wages are unaffordable. Corporate balance sheets have been healthy. Decent pay accorded workers is returned in expanded customer bases. Recent research is showing that cities' living wage laws, rather than triggering the job losses some economists had predicted, are causing few job cutbacks and in fact are lifting many families out of poverty.

Can cities lead? Austin Mayor Kirk Watson believes they should lead by example in their regions to help low-wage workers move into family-supporting jobs.

Austin itself raised all city workers to $8 an hour. And that's just a first step, says Watson, in his or any city tackling major unfinished business in the new century.

A "Living Wage" Will Not Eliminate Poverty

Nathan Karp

In the following selection, Nathan Karp examines the "living wage" movement, which he describes as an attempt to eradicate poverty among a select group of workers. As he explains, the movement's supporters encourage communities to pass local ordinances requiring companies that have government contracts to pay their workers at a much higher rate than the federal minimum wage. According to Karp, supporters of the living wage movement hope that the local ordinances will help workers to better support their families and will ultimately lead to the establishment of a federal living wage. However, Karp points out, these laws only affect a few workers who are employed by businesses with city contracts. The majority of the working poor will not benefit from these limited laws, he concludes. Karp is a writer for *The People*, the monthly newspaper of the Socialist Labor Party of America.

Poverty has long been a constant of capitalist United States, despite many efforts by government agencies and private organizations to wipe it out. Those efforts not only have failed to eliminate poverty, they failed even to ameliorate it in any substantive degree. President Lyndon B. Johnson's much-ballyhooed and government-sponsored "War on Poverty" provides a case in point.

A New Antipoverty Effort

Now comes a new antipoverty effort. This one, too, is being bally-hooed and sponsored by government bodies, but this time primarily at the city level. It is part of a movement already operating in many states. It does not pretend to aim at achieving the total elimination of poverty—at least not at this stage of its efforts. Rather it has the limited objective of wiping out poverty among workers employed by contractors who have or seek contracts with the city. It aims to accomplish that by convincing the cities to set a local minimum-wage

From "Municipal 'Living Wage' Movement Built on Illusions," by Nathan Karp, *The People*, March 1999. Copyright © 1999 by Nathan Karp. Reprinted with permission.

requirement which firms working for the city must meet.

The first city to establish such minimum wage was Baltimore in 1994. The federal minimum wage then was under $5. The city mandated a "new" minimum wage for companies that had contracts with the city. The Baltimore minimum was set at $6.10 an hour with the further proviso that it rise to $7.70 by July 1998. After that date, the city's minimum wage would be adjusted for inflation. These new "living wage" minimums were expected to enable a *working* mother with one child to maintain a standard of living above the "official" poverty line. However, a worker with a wife and two children (the so-called average American family) earning the city's minimum wage would remain in poverty, well below the "officially" designated national poverty line. As Robert Pollin, an economics professor at the University of Massachusetts-Amherst, noted in a recent article, "Baltimore's 'living wage' . . . is not much of a living. . . ."

There are 18 cities—including such major cities as New York, Los Angeles, Chicago and Boston—that have enacted "living wage" minimums; and demands for such minimums are being pressed in 23 additional cities. Not all the cities set the same minimums. No doubt local conditions, political considerations, the general state of the labor market, etc., have their effects. The highest minimum wage that city contractors must pay was set by the San Jose, Calif., city council in November 1998—$9.50 an hour with health benefits or $10.75 an hour without health benefits. It is claimed that as a result "hundreds" of San Jose workers will now escape from poverty. Even if true, that amounts to a small percentage of the total number of San Jose workers and their families still trapped in poverty, even though probably most of those families have at least one employed member. And that is very likely true in every one of the cities establishing such local minimum wages.

In 1997 there were 7.3 million families in the nation officially designated as poor. Yet the majority—66 percent or close to 5 million of those families—each had at least one jobholder in the family. A number of those pushing for these limited minimum-wage provisions at the city level are aware that those limited gains will affect the poverty numbers "only modestly." They are hoping, however, that the effort at the city level will lead to something greater—specifically, a national minimum wage that will make a "living wage" a reality for the majority of all families still existing in poverty. The national minimum wage being suggested is $7.25 an hour. That is over 30 percent less than the minimum set by the city of San Jose. It is even 5.5 percent less than the $7.70 goal set by the city of Baltimore in 1994.

The "living wage" advocates also contend that the "successes" at the city level will prove to be a boost in several other ways. Thus, Madeline Janis-Aparicio, director of the Los Angeles Living Wage Coalition, says the "living wage" movement is also "a tool for union organizing, for confronting the problem of wage inequality and for expressing a certain level of dignified treatment of workers."

The Laws of Supply and Demand

Eighty-eight years ago, a then "leading Jesuit," Father Thomas I. Gasson, delivered a widely circulated attack on socialism in which he admonished the capitalists that labor should not be treated as a "bale of merchandise." He then quoted the following from an encyclical letter issued by Pope Leo XIII. "No capitalist should fail to give the toilers a wage which would enable the toiler to live in decent circumstances." Daniel De Leon answered the attack in a series of articles in the *Daily People*, in which he demonstrated that under capitalism labor is indeed a "merchandise" and, as such, its wage, i.e., price, is subject to the supply and demand for labor in the labor market. In accordance with this economic fact, De Leon then noted:

> Whosoever advocates capitalism, and yet demands that the workingman be well paid and be not allowed to be treated as a bale of merchandise, cuts, on the field of sociology, a figure no less ridiculous, not to say suspicious, than he would cut on the field of zoology if he praised a tiger, and yet sought to make people believe that the beast could be made to bleat like a lamb, and to delight in sugared water, instead of red, hot blood fresh from the gashes it inflicts.

The drive for the so-called "living wage" may get increases of a couple of dollars for a small percentage of workers employed by firms with city contracts. But, by and large, the wages of the great majority in those cities will continue to be determined by the economic laws of capitalism.

WELFARE REFORM IS HELPING THE POOR MOVE OUT OF POVERTY

Aimee Howd

The passage of the Personal Responsibility and Work Opportunity Act in 1996 dramatically altered the regulations concerning the distribution of welfare benefits. The most significant changes in the welfare reform law included new limits on the length of time welfare recipients could receive benefits and the requirement that all healthy, able-bodied recipients work in public service jobs. In the following article, Aimee Howd maintains that these reforms have been successful in drastically reducing the number of people who receive government assistance. The new emphasis on helping welfare recipients to learn good work skills and find jobs is far more effective than simply providing the needy with government handouts, Howd asserts. Welfare reform is succeeding, she claims, because it provides the poor with the help they need to change their lives on a permanent basis. Howd is a writer for *Insight on the News*, a conservative weekly magazine.

Cash-assistance caseloads have plunged roughly 40 percent across the country since 1994, and spirits are soaring among those who believe America's welfare programs at last are giving the nation's needy a hand up instead of just a handout. "The look of welfare has changed," says Michael Kharfen, speaking for the U.S. Department of Health and Human Services, or HHS. "Now welfare offices look more like employment centers."

Welfare to Work

Caseworkers used to be concerned with determining the size of the government check for which an aid applicant could qualify. Now, Kharfen says, they are "trying to get people into work—teaching them how to interview, how to dress, how to fill out application forms, requiring them to go out and do a certain number of job interviews a day."

The revised system worked for Cassandra Tucker. In 1998 this 27-

year-old had just given birth to her sixth child and was out of work. Like all Wisconsin residents, she knew that applying for public assistance meant applying for a job. Welfare had passed away and been reincarnated as Wisconsin Works, or W2, the most radical welfare-to-work program in the nation.

A YWCA-based agency had been chosen to manage the local work program. Tucker polished her workplace skills and habits through YW Works. Before long, Genevieve Kukla, president of an inner-city Milwaukee manufacturing and construction company, called the agency looking for workers. Tucker interviewed and became one of 925 people in 1998 who landed jobs instead of welfare checks through YW Works.

To her evident amazement, April 1999 found Tucker testifying in welfare-reform hearings before the House Committee on Government Reform alongside her boss, Kukla, and the executive director of the YWCA Women Enterprise Center, Julia Taylor. "Some aspects of W2 are positive, some negative. But it's the people you meet along the way that determine the positive or negative," Tucker told House leaders. Motioning toward her boss she added, "Ms. Kukla has been very supportive."

These three women say a lot about the system that is replacing welfare handouts throughout the nation: a solidly planned state program managed at the local level, working with employers and community supporters to tap the resources of people who have lost—or never found—their way. "The environment is characterized by a new culture in which innovation and reform are rewarded, as is individual achievement and effort," says Taylor.

Where welfare reform is working best in the nation it is because of what its critics call a "paternalistic policy." This involves setting reasonable and enforceable expectations that encourage responsible behavior. (W2 benefits ultimately are not contingent upon need but upon the number of hours actually worked.) It also requires giving a helping hand up from the miseries of inadequate training, transportation, child care and health services. (Wisconsin's social benefits for the needy are second to none. The latest hype surrounds building state-of-the-art child-development centers for at-risk children, replete with speakers to pipe in foreign languages and classical music.)

Hiring people out of welfare is becoming normal business practice in this time of nearly full employment. Studies are showing a high level of retention once workers settle into jobs. Tucker is one of three W2 workers Kukla has on her small staff—she says she will train anyone willing to take on all the responsibility they can handle. It's both a labor of love and a business venture for her. "Someone has to care," says Kukla, affectionately remembering two times that Tucker walked out on the job, only to call back and apologize. "You have to give them responsibility and tell them, 'Look I need you and I am depending on you,'" says Kukla. Her forbearance has paid off, and today Tucker is working her way up to construction-project manager.

The first lesson is the basic discipline of showing up for work, Kukla says. Thus, some states require recipients who aren't ready for employment to perform volunteer work in exchange for support. This seems to be working. The economics of it are clear enough: While liberals historically reacted against the concept of asking people to leave welfare for a minimum-wage job, experts note that the average welfare recipient is 30 percent below the national poverty line, and even a minimum-wage job will put them 30 percent above that line.

Changing the Face of Welfare

On a national level, who deserves credit for the changing face of welfare? During his 1992 presidential campaign Bill Clinton promised to "end welfare as we know it." But he then proceeded in his first budget to ask for a $100 billion increase over five years in welfare spending. In addition, not only did he fail to develop work programs for welfare recipients, he undermined the minimal work requirements in the existing law.

Perhaps the most substantial initiative of the Clinton administration was to grant waivers to states whose innovative programs were at odds with restrictions on the federal entitlement dollars they distributed. Observers on both sides of the political aisle suggest these waivers at the state level may be responsible for the fact that the welfare rolls began their steady decline in 1993. But the very fact that waivers were necessary highlighted the labyrinthine nature of the federal regulatory system. Ultimately, they represented only variations on the old theme of an inefficient, centralized welfare bureaucracy.

The Republican-dominated 104th Congress challenged Clinton in 1995 to put feet to his rhetoric. After twice vetoing their welfare-reform legislation—and with his own reelection bid looming—Clinton signed the 1996 Personal Responsibility and Work Opportunity Act, a conservative legislative victory that entirely altered the national welfare debate.

The metamorphosis is crystallized in the title of the cash-assistance program. What had been the Aid to Families with Dependent Children, or AFDC, since Lyndon B. Johnson declared war on poverty 30 years ago, became the Temporary Assistance to Needy Families, or TANF.

First there was a movement of control from the federal to the state level. Under AFDC, federal monies were tied to state caseloads and, thus, states that decreased dependency were penalized. Under TANF, federal block grants are given and any surplus federal funds resulting from caseload reduction can be kept by the states for use in other efforts to aid the poor. Some states are funneling their savings to increase support for the hardest-to-help families—providing care for sick children or substance-abuse treatment—while others are setting aside the money for a rainy day, lest a downturn in the economy result in massive layoffs of the newly placed workers.

Also, states were given greater flexibility, especially when it comes to tying work requirements to welfare dollars. A study by the conservative Heritage Foundation links declines in state welfare rolls directly to the work requirements they impose.

The federal government retained the right to hold states accountable for meeting goals for employment and reduced dependence. In one of its most controversial measures, it established limits of 24 consecutive months of federal benefits and five years as the maximum lifetime benefit per household. In two other changes, out-of-wedlock births (now at one-third of all American children born) were recognized as a cause of growing welfare dependency, and bonuses were promised to states that reduce illegitimacy. Faith-based organizations were given the right to contract for delivery of services to needy families without compromising their religious character.

On April 9, 1999, HHS announced "new caseload figures showing more parents moving into the workforce with 7.6 million recipients left on the rolls as of December 1998, a decline of 38 percent since 1993, 46 percent since the law was signed in 1996." Since 1993, caseloads in 29 states have fallen by half or more. Sixty percent of households leaving cash assistance are moving directly into jobs.

The other 40 percent are more difficult to track. Experts say we aren't seeing families sleeping on the streets, as some critics of the legislation suggested would happen, but anecdotal indicators including huge increases in visits to religious food pantries demonstrate that the need hasn't just disappeared.

Declining Caseloads

Wendell Primus, who responded to the new welfare approach by resigning his post as assistant secretary at HHS, wrote recently, "The conventional wisdom is welfare reform is working because welfare caseloads have declined sharply. . . . But any assessment of the success of the welfare-reform law should take into account . . . evidence of whether welfare reform has improved, or at minimum, held harmless the economic circumstances of poor, single-mother families." He calls for increased social supports and more analysis of national data.

This drive for more data collection reflects the still-pervasive fear among social workers and other professional liberals that, without strict federal oversight, states will race for the bottom line without concern for the suffering of the poor. But state governments believe they've proved themselves and say the greatest drag on their burgeoning reforms is the burdensome paperwork the federal government still requires.

With caseloads down, most states are spending substantially more per capita on families in workfare than they spent on families who were drawing government checks for nothing. This appeals to grass-roots public opinion, says Lawrence Mead of New York University, one of the nation's most respected experts on political aspects of poverty and welfare. Public opinion almost uniformly favors a welfare policy that is both "generous and demanding," he says. "The political mystery has never been why we now have the national policies we have, but why we didn't have them 30 years ago."

Before the 1996 legislation, says the Center for Public Justice's Stanley Carlson-Thies, author of several books on welfare-related policy, an irreconcilable polarization existed along conservative and liberal lines. "One side was saying here are a lot of needy people—we have to give them everything they need. The other side was saying aid will make them dependent, take it away and let them swim for themselves. This legislation represents a package of new thinking about welfare. It got through the polarity. It said people need help, but the help they need is the kind to help them get their lives together."

Of course, some say the Republican legislation had no impact, that the booming economy and other Clinton social policies are responsible for the change. It's statistically difficult to confirm anything other than the raw numbers. The results from state to state vary as widely as the innovations they are attempting. In many cases, the discrepancies are glaring even from county to county as states have chosen to allow local communities to administer their own reforms.

Florida's Work and Gain Economic Self-Sufficiency workfare program, for example, is governed by 24 local coalitions overseen by a state board governed by a majority of private leaders. Florida has led the nation's eight largest states in welfare-caseload declines. Only 1 percent of the families subject to time limits when the program began in 1996 reached their 1998 deadline. Michael Poole, chairman of the board of directors, sums up Florida's reform philosophy as "local control, local responsibility."

A New Day

But, of course, nowhere is the welfare-reform outlook more optimistic than Wisconsin, where three-term Republican Gov. Tommy Thompson officially ended welfare in 1996 by signing the W2 program into law. The reforms cut caseloads from a high of around 100,000 to about 8,800 by the spring of 1999—a historic decline of more than 91 percent.

"A new day has dawned in America. The nation's states, America's true laboratories of democracy, were empowered to break the devastating cycle of dependence and poverty that 60 years of welfare entitlements have wrought upon this country. And no state epitomizes the success of American welfare reform more than my own state of Wisconsin," boasted Thompson before a quiet crowd of policymakers, political analysts, government social workers and leaders of private charities gathered in May 1999 at Washington's National Press Club for talks on "The Next Steps in Welfare Reform," sponsored by the Manhattan Institute. Indeed, Wisconsin's reform efforts, begun under waivers from the federal government, helped inspire the 1996 federal welfare-reform act. And they continue to set the tone for the national debate.

But AFDC was the only means-tested government benefit program to get a substantial overhaul. And it is one of 70 separate federal-aid programs. In 1998, in fact, in spite of the reforms in cash assistance, total federal and state spending on welfare programs including food stamps, health benefits and housing assistance remained at a near-record high of $400 billion. That amounts to about 5 percent of the gross domestic product and a tax burden of $5,000 on the average American family.

"The changes within AFDC were quite significant, but both proponents and detractors of the reform have made it sound more dramatic than it actually was," says Robert Rector, a demographics expert for the Heritage Foundation. "The 1996 reforms were certainly not an end to welfare; you have to put them in the context of the overall welfare system."

Of the 8,800 households still on cash assistance in Wisconsin, 80 percent are in the urban Milwaukee area, an indication that the next steps in welfare reform likely will involve the "urban underclass," where unemployment has been virulent, positive role models are scarce and absent fathers have left cycles of crime and substance abuse in their wakes.

As Rep. Clay Shaw, a Florida Republican, noted in 1998, "To take the next step in welfare reform, we must find a way to help children by providing them with more than a working mother and sporadic child support. . . . Welfare reform has changed the rules for mothers—work has replaced dependency. Now it's time for marriage to replace illegitimacy. Given the repeated failure of large-scale government social interventions, we must begin this fight where it eventually will be won—in the neighborhoods where young boys grow up to be fathers but not husbands."

THE MIXED RESULTS OF WELFARE REFORM

Christina Duff

Christina Duff, a staff reporter for the *Wall Street Journal*, examines the mixed results of welfare reform in the following article. Duff explains that many people who left the welfare rolls are now working at jobs that do not pay enough to lift them above the poverty level. She also notes that people who give up welfare may lose important and costly benefits, such as health insurance, since these benefits are not included in most low-wage jobs. Former welfare recipients who have made the transition to work often find it difficult to survive without a safety net, she writes. Duff concludes that while welfare reform did significantly reduce the number of people on welfare and did put more people to work, it also appears to have made little difference in the quality of life experienced by the poor.

Sara Day could be considered a welfare-reform success story.

After 10 years on welfare, she has a two-year-college degree and earns $11-an-hour as a secretary at a prep school. Her welfare cash and food stamps stopped in 1998, and her government-paid health care ended in 1999. Her only major tether is medical care for her children.

So why is the tiny, soft-spoken, 28-year-old, single mom contemplating a return to welfare?

Because her take-home pay and child support total $1,435.50 a month, and food, rent and other basic expenses total $1,418.37, not counting clothing, diapers or pills for her migraines. To make ends meet, she lets bills go unpaid and sends her children to day care even when she isn't working so they can get the free lunch. She has no health insurance, and her partially subsidized rent is climbing faster than her paychecks.

In 1997, she told the *Wall Street Journal*, approvingly, that welfare reform was "getting people up off their butts." Today, as she thinks of asking her mother's church for help and contemplates quitting her job for a lower-paying one that would hoist her back on the rolls, Ms.

Day says, "I would like to know what the advantages are supposed to be of being off welfare."

Limited Child Support

Her situation is exacerbated by the fact that she has five children between the ages of two months and 12 years, but collects child support for only two. Although only 10% of families on welfare in September 1997 had four or more children, Ms. Day's circumstances aren't unusual. Two of the toughest challenges to "ending welfare as we know it," as President Bill Clinton promised, are finding ways to reward work while still protecting the children of low-wage workers and forcing deadbeat dads to support their children.

Ms. Day is a face behind the statistics cited both by welfare-reform supporters and critics. Her family is one of about 1.6 million families that have left the welfare rolls between 1996 and 1999, and she is one of those cited in state surveys that find up to 70% of former recipients have found work. Low-wage workers are enjoying solid raises at last, and the federal earned-income tax credit is supplementing their income, as it is Ms. Day's.

Americans should stop escalating what they consider to be an acceptable standard of living, argues Robert Rector of the conservative Heritage Foundation. "We see a single mother whose income is above the average income of a family in the '50s, yet we now decide she's having a hard time," he says.

But Rebecca Blank, a member of President Clinton's Council of Economic Advisers, says, "It's not just about getting a job, any job. We have to think about how to help people survive while working."

A study by the Institute for Wisconsin's Future suggests that welfare reform may be more successful at moving low-income families off welfare rolls than lifting them out of poverty. The liberal nonprofit group found that the number of welfare recipients in Wisconsin decreased by 67% between 1986 and 1997, but that the number of people in poverty fell by only 11.8%. Wisconsin launched its welfare reform effort in 1986.

Ms. Day's job has several drawbacks. She works only 30 hours a week and the temporary employment agency that pays her doesn't provide any benefits. But the job is uniquely accommodating. Ms. Day receives day-care vouchers from the state of Ohio, but no facility will take an infant under three months. So she wheels her two-month-old through the prep school's hallways to work each day.

From her desk drawer, Ms. Day pulls the newspaper wants ads, some highlighted: data entry worker, a lawyer's assistant, all for longer hours. But she would get home after 5 p.m., and that would mean leaving her eldest son Chris, who will lose eligibility for day care when he turns 13, home alone for a couple of hours each day.

Her current job, at least, gives her flexibility. Her boss, Antoinette Hubbard, has placed a pile of envelopes on her desk to be stuffed and addressed. "You know," Ms. Day says, glancing at the clock, "I have to be out of here by 3."

"I understand," Ms. Hubbard chirps.

Marrying a man with a paycheck would help, but she says she "couldn't stand" the father of her first son, and the father of the next two ended up in jail. She hoped she might marry the man she says fathered her youngest two, "but, of course, that's not going to happen," Ms. Day says with a short, humorless laugh. He accepts paternity and pays support for only one of the two kids.

If the men are so unfit, why keep having children? That's more complicated. As the youngest of seven children of a welfare recipient whose husband deserted her, Ms. Day admired the families her siblings were starting. "I'd see babies in the park and say, 'I want one with a whole bunch of black hair,'" Ms. Day says, smiling wanly. "And that's what I did, I guess."

Her children provide her with a sense of accomplishment that the job never will. "Will you ever have a baby that isn't beautiful?" a coworker asks, bending over the crib to ogle the blue-eyed infant.

Back at her three-bedroom brick home after work, Ms. Day sits at the kitchen table as her children study. One by one they show her their homework; if she nods, they dash to play outside.

Ms. Day rents the house under a program in which the local housing authority covers the difference between the tenant's payments and the rent a landlord would get on the open market. At first, the housing authority first charged her a small percentage of her pretax income, adjusted for the size of her family. But after a year, the rent shot up to 30% of her pretax income, the standard rate. Monthly rent is now $526, still below the market-value rent of $700. Welfare officials are discussing additional housing subsidies to families like the Days.

To make ends meet, Ms. Day cuts costs. During a recent special on Hamburger Helper, she piled it high in her cupboard. But there's no money for meat. There are no donuts, no fruit snacks, no treats. When eight-year-old James displays a green apple Jolly Rancher stick he got at school, his mother tells him to eat it in another room so the other kids won't feel bad.

It's not that she doesn't think welfare reform is a good idea. "I'm glad to be off," Ms. Day says. "I'm sure a lot of people out there are just sitting at home, waiting for that once-a-month check to come in. This would motivate them people."

Yet she wonders: What is the point of going to work if she can't even buy the basics? If she worked fewer hours, perhaps the government would give back her medical benefits. Or if she took a job with lesser pay, her rent would diminish. Certainly, being back on the rolls would ease her stress.

"This thing was supposed to work," Ms. Day says. "It's not. And it doesn't make any sense."

WORKFARE: SUCCESSES AND FAILURES

Heather MacDonald

The Personal Responsibility and Work Opportunity Act of 1996 instituted a new program known as workfare that requires able-bodied recipients to perform public-service jobs in exchange for their benefits. In the following article, Heather MacDonald reports on the successes and failures of two government-sponsored welfare-to-work programs in New York City and Wisconsin. According to MacDonald, these programs do provide beneficial job training for many welfare recipients, especially in the areas of self-discipline and socialization. However, she notes, other recipients are simply not able to meet the demands placed on them by the workfare programs. She also points out that Wisconsin's workfare programs have been far more successful in rural counties than in the impoverished urban neighborhoods of Milwaukee. MacDonald is a writer for the quarterly magazine *City Journal*.

If the architects of welfare reform ever harbor doubts about the future success of their plans, people like Lisa and Rhafel McElrath must haunt their dreams. Will the new federal law that makes welfare recipients work for their checks reverse the passivity and degradation the old system has entrenched over the last 30 years? It's much too soon to know. But couples like the McElraths suggest how monumental the task of reclamation will be.

Late in October 1996, Rhafel, 33, fidgeted in the hallway of a New York City Parks Department building in East Harlem while Lisa received her orientation for the city's workfare program. Tall and well built, sporting a trendy Tommy Hilfiger Collection sweatshirt and a gold earring, Rhafel quickly changes the subject when I ask why Lisa, not he, will start working for the couple's welfare check tomorrow. Pressed further, he takes his stand on principle: "I'll have to like the job I'm doing. And I won't work for less than minimum wage."

Lisa and Rhafel are the end products of one of the more perverse schemes for social improvement designed by man. They live on Home Relief, a state- and city-funded program for able-bodied childless adults that is virtually identical in both its benefit levels and its destructive consequences to Aid to Families with Dependent Children (AFDC), the main federal welfare program. Devoid of personal initiative, they define their lives wholly by the welfare entitlements that surround them. Move to another state? Only if the welfare system there will support them. Look for work? Sorry, not compatible with their gypsy life in the city's homeless shelter system, which requires them to move every month. While in some respects easy, such an existence is by no means simple. They are at the mercy of faulty computers, incompetent bureaucrats, arbitrary rules, and periodic changes in their welfare case that they may or may not deserve but almost never comprehend. "I'm getting very sick of this," Rhafel petulantly says, as if he has no other choices. . . .

Twenty-eight now, Lisa has worked only once—14 years ago in a summer youth job. She doesn't get along well with people, she explains; also, she has hypertension and takes medication for a mental disorder. As we leave the Parks building and her partner disappears to do an errand, Lisa explains why she, not Rhafel, will be working tomorrow: "Because he's lazy," she says decisively. But why not make him head of the welfare case, so he has to do the workfare program? She taps her head meaningfully: "I may be slow, but I'm not stupid." Like many underclass women, she has opted for the security of welfare over the sure disaster of a shiftless man—a shiftlessness that the welfare ethic is at least partly responsible for perpetuating.

The New Welfare Rules

When Congress voted in July 1996 to abolish AFDC, it hoped to smash the dependency culture that defines Rhafel and Lisa McElrath's lives. It ended the entitlement status of federal welfare programs, meaning that the federal government will no longer guarantee assistance to everyone who meets its criteria for neediness. No provision struck greater fear and loathing into the hearts of poverty lobbyists, for they realized its potential to shift the ground of all social policy from a rights-based system of claims on government to one of mutual obligation: to get a government benefit, you now must do something in return. Equally abhorrent to the advocate bloc is the moral message of abolishing AFDC: you have no unconditional claim on your neighbors' support if you have an illegitimate child.

In lieu of automatic federal welfare payments, Congress created a system of block grants to the states. States will now determine who should receive aid and for how long, using the federal money to supplement their own programs. For now, state definitions of welfare eligibility aren't likely to change markedly, but over the long run states may decide that teen mothers, say, are not eligible for cash assistance, or may require them to live in group homes to get benefits.

Two aspects of the new law will have an immediate impact, however: its work requirements and time limits on federal aid.

The work requirement is hardly new in America. For two centuries before the activism of welfare-rights advocacy and the explosive growth of AFDC distorted the system, the able-bodied had to work in exchange for aid. The new law reinstates the requirement, penalizing states financially if they don't put a rising portion of their welfare recipients to work. The new law won't require welfare grantees to work right away; it allows a two-year period of idleness (which states may override) and gives states a six-year grace period until they have to put just half their caseload to work.

The most controversial aspect of the bill is its five-year lifetime limit on federal aid for any given family. An exemption of 20 percent of a state's caseload, a percentage roughly equal to the irremediably dysfunctional population, softens the federal limit, and states remain free to use their own money for support beyond the five years. Nevertheless, the time limit is crucial: today, across the entire national welfare caseload, the average cumulative length of stay is 13 years, with plenty of 15- and 20-year spells on the rolls. The time limit, more than anything else, should push states to move recipients aggressively toward independence.

The law will spark change on an unprecedented scale, but local welfare reform efforts make it possible to predict some likely results. The centerpiece of reform thus far has been workfare, and two places—New York City and the state of Wisconsin—have led the national effort to put welfare recipients to work. New York's is a largely untold story, while Wisconsin, which organizes workfare very differently, has become a symbol of aggressive reform. Taken together, both stories demonstrate the strengths and limitations of workfare. While putting people to work is a necessary prerequisite to rebuilding character, it only *begins* the moral reconstruction of the inner city.

Welfare Reform in New York City

New York City is the sleeper of welfare reform. Despite its well-earned reputation as the nation's dependency capital, it is actually making giant changes in its fossilized welfare culture. It is putting into practice key lessons learned 20 years ago in the aftermath of the welfare-rights revolution. Following the advocacy-inspired surge in the welfare rolls in the seventies, the state and city imposed stricter welfare eligibility tests and work requirements. Officials discovered that for every trivial hurdle put between a recipient and his welfare check, a very non-trivial portion of the caseload simply disappears. Pick up your welfare check in person? Too much trouble. In the late seventies, welfare commissioner Blanche Bernstein ordered individuals on Home Relief to participate in government-operated workfare. The refusal rate ranged from 21 percent to 40 percent, demonstrating that many welfare recipients already work and cannot be in two places at once. . . .

The centerpiece of the administration's welfare reform effort is its huge workfare program, called the Work Experience Program, or WEP. It is unique among the nation's current workfare experiments in its massive creation of public sector jobs: 35,000 welfare recipients, consisting of all new applicants and an increasing proportion of existing cases, the great majority on Home Relief, are currently sweeping the city's streets, cleaning its courthouses, and tending its parks. City Hall will have to increase that number to approximately 60,000 by 1997 to meet the requirements of the new federal welfare bill—a daunting task. One thing that immediately strikes a visitor to the city's WEP sites is that the program is not make-work. WEP workers are doing desperately needed maintenance tasks. They are cleaning jury rooms neglected for years, painting and repairing broken park furniture, and removing great swaths of graffiti. Street cleanliness ratings are setting records.

Trying to Instill the Work Ethic

It has fallen to city employees to try to instill the work ethic in people who either have long since lost it or, like the McElraths, never had it. Reggie Washington, a WEP supervisor in Central Park, is just about ideal for that task. Small, round-faced, and wearing a diamond stud in one ear, he acquired his views on work and welfare from his feverishly disciplined Cuban mother and his travels abroad. "In Africa," he says, "if you don't work, you don't eat. These people here don't know how good they've got it." He cites the contents of the current welfare package—free phone installation, food stamps, a housing allowance, and Medicaid—in wonder. "I've got a guy who got out of prison after ten years, and now he's getting benefits," he muses incredulously.

One cold October morning, Washington herds a group of WEP workers into a green Parks Department van and rumbles off with them to Fifth Avenue and 60th Street. There the workers tumble out, seize their tools, and immediately start raking and bagging leaves and trash. The alacrity and efficiency with which they begin working is the fruit of three weeks of training. For many, this is their first socialization to work. "Sometimes I have to send people home for bad language or street habits," Washington says. "This is work; I'm not going to tolerate that." Workers sent home have to make up the time. WEP sites try to maintain strict lateness policies and to enforce a modest dress code as well. Workers with unexcused absences get cut from the program and may lose their grants for a period of time.

The crew itself is a key source of socialization. Washington recalls that one crew threatened to beat up a fellow worker who was so lazy that he was holding it back. The women on Washington's current crew recently had a "little talk" with an extraordinarily hostile fellow worker about her attitude—she had screamed at me, for example, that workfare was "indentured servitude." Now she has settled down and become a good worker.

For many welfare recipients, the demands of the WEP program, including simply getting to work on time, are impossible to meet. The attrition rate is high. Up to 50 percent of recipients never show up for their first WEP orientation; after that, many supervisors lose 10 to 15 percent of their workers every two weeks.

Malik Medora, a slight, pale 19-year-old with a few bristles on his chin, is one of those who didn't make it. Raised in Children's Village, a large foster home in Dobbs Ferry, New York, Medora is a homeless orphan, his mother having died of drug use and his father of drug-related AIDS. He spent his teens in the Coxsackie detention center near the Catskills for robbery, burglary, assaulting a police officer, and resisting arrest. Most of his brothers and sisters ended up in jail as well. He is currently trying to assemble a wardrobe, in part by theft. The possibility of getting caught holds no terrors for him: "At least if I go to jail, I'll have three meals a day," he sighs during a break from his park WEP job. A ninth-grade dropout, Medora has been filling out job applications, but he has no address or phone number to give employers.

When I spoke to him, Medora expressed gratitude for the WEP program. "This is constructive," he said. "It gets me experience." Less than two weeks later, he went AWOL. When welfare advocates insist that the city should be investing huge additional sums in job training for welfare recipients, it is well to bear in mind that many of the trainees, like Medora, are so far from job-ready that the investment will go down the drain. Medora needs help, to be sure, but job training doesn't address his problems.

"A Great Experience"

For those many other WEP workers ready for work—estimates range from a quarter to a third of the caseload—the program offers a small but real step into the job market. Supervisors quickly learn the work habits of their workers, and many go out of their way to provide some additional training, as well as job references, for the good workers. Omar Williams, a slender, remarkably polite 32-year-old, went from Reggie Washington's WEP crew to a maintenance job with the Central Park Conservancy. "It was a great experience," Williams says of the WEP program.

His enthusiasm is not an aberration. Many WEP workers appreciate the chance to do something useful. An older woman on Home Relief for the first time told me, "They shoulda done this long ago. It's a fair deal and valuable work. Some people sit there and do nothing and take advantage of the system." Some WEPs volunteer extra hours and take pride in their work, especially if they are stationed close to home and neighbors can see the results of their efforts.

Other WEP workers, however, seethe with indignation. Unlike other cities' workfare programs, WEP makes little attempt to place people according to their skills, and recipients with work histories often feel insulted by being asked to clean streets. The city should be finding them jobs, they say, not "exploiting" their labor. . . .

Thoughtful critics question whether workfare should take the form of a vast government jobs program. Many welfare experts, for instance, argue that large public employment programs like WEP are impossibly expensive. . . .

Other critics cite the risk that government workfare jobs will become an entitlement, "just another form of welfare," in Wisconsin governor Tommy Thompson's phrase. People doing workfare, these critics say, can grow satisfied with their duties and feel little imperative to find private work. This charge has real bite. WEP supervisors already notice a tendency among good workers who enjoy their jobs to settle in for the long haul. The threat of time limits may, in the future, change that, but the city will also have to step up its nascent efforts to push people into the private sector.

If New York does increase its job placement efforts, according to another set of skeptics, it might well find that public-sector workfare is dead-end work, offering no bridge to the private economy. How many employers are looking for street cleaners or snow shovelers? But this criticism misses the point. Specific job skills are not the issue; socialization and discipline are. . . .

The Wisconsin Program

Half a continent away, Wisconsin, which welfare gurus laud as the foremost reform laboratory in the country, takes a diametrically opposite approach to workfare. No New York City–style public jobs program for it. Instead, Wisconsin puts welfare recipients to work in private- and nonprofit-sector jobs. Visitors stream into the state to see the system in action—to learn about Wisconsin's one-stop job centers, its diversion of applicants to non-welfare sources of support, and its so-called "pay-for-performance" model of workfare. Even the new federal law incorporates several of its reforms. Yet for all its successes, Wisconsin has had some disappointments, with serious implications for the adequacy of workfare as a tool of cultural renewal. And even the successes have only limited applicability to the inner-city populations that reformers worry about most, for they take place in rural areas where the scale of the welfare problem is minuscule compared to that of the South Bronx or Watts.

Wisconsin has been working at welfare reform longer than any other state. Between 1987, when Governor Tommy Thompson came into office vowing to stem the growing welfare crisis, and 1994, the state's caseload dropped 23 percent, more than double the nation's next largest decline. In some rural counties, the rolls dropped more than 70 percent over the seven years. However remarkable this may seem, it's important to remember that the state's robust economy, very different from New York's, made much of the reduction possible.

Many Wisconsin counties have virtually no unemployment; companies are desperate for workers. But though the rolls surely would have dropped on their own, they wouldn't have dropped as far without the state's radical changes in policy.

The big idea at the heart of Wisconsin's reform is to get recipients off welfare fast—or, better yet, to dissuade applicants from coming on in the first place, a concept known as "diversion." Welfare department planners meet with an applicant before she even applies for assistance to analyze her budget, consider alternative sources of support—such as WIC [Women, Infants, and Children, a supplemental program], Medicaid, or soon, no-interest government loans—and to drive home the reality of the welfare work requirement. Equally important, applicants must spend 60 hours looking for work before seeing their first check.

In rural areas, this strategy has produced remarkable results. During a two-week period in Fond-du-Lac County, a dairy and light-manufacturing county in the middle of the state and the site of the state's most far-reaching welfare experiments to date, 16 people came into the county's welfare office to apply for support; only two ended up doing so, having been proselytized by the county's welfare workers to the new state religion of self-sufficiency. Much of Wisconsin's welfare bureaucracy is possessed by an almost holy zeal to move people into employment.

Job-Readiness Activities

If diversion fails, Wisconsin immediately throws recipients into a flurry of activity designed to place them in jobs. If the pre-application job search has produced no offers, the client must enroll immediately in a daily program of job-readiness training, community service, or highly focused short-term job training. In Fond-du-Lac, for instance, the county provides two- to six-week courses in such skills as welding, printing, and nursing assistance. The smaller counties also provide customized service for the required work component: welfare workers phone local employers looking for an opening that matches a recipient's interests.

Wisconsin makes its job-readiness activities as job-like as possible with a "pay-for-performance" system. For every hour of unexcused absence from a job search program or a community service placement, a participant's check is docked $4.25. Result: in Fond-du-Lac, almost a third of the county's caseload opted to give up their welfare checks rather than participate in the intensely supervised job-readiness and workfare program. With predictable illogic, welfare advocates argue that this high rate of attrition shows that Wisconsin's reforms aren't working, as if the only acceptable reforms are those that keep people safely ensconced on the rolls.

Many welfare recipients, some of them migrants from large cities, are angry, too, about the reforms—just as angry as recipients in New

York. I spoke with a middle-aged woman in the jobs center of Kenosha County, a reform showcase midway between Milwaukee and Chicago, who had been called in for quitting her telemarketing job after three days. "They make me sick—fuck them!" she spat out, after drawing heavily on a cigarette. "I do not understand why you would ask me to volunteer four hours a day and not pay me wages. It's slavery. I refuse!" The woman, a former postal worker who wouldn't say why she left her government job, is part of a large migration of inner-city Chicagoans who came to Wisconsin for its welfare benefits. Faced with the state's new workfare regime, many are now returning to Chicago. "They are trying to enforce work in Chicago," the woman explained, "but there's so many welfare recipients that it's hard to get them. It's still easier to find loopholes there."

In one of the most significant experiments for the new federal bill, two Wisconsin counties, Fond-du-Lac and Pierce, instituted a two-year time limit on welfare in January 1995. By October 1996, most Fond-du-Lac recipients were off the rolls, leaving only two people facing the mandatory cutoff in December. But after two years of getting the able-bodied off welfare, the county is left with a markedly changed clientele. More and more of those coming up to the mandatory cutoff in the months to come will be the truly dysfunctional. Some have mild mental illness or a low I.Q.; others, according to Roger Kowtz, a state project manager, "simply don't have a clue." When the county finds jobs for such individuals, they quickly get fired for absenteeism, tardiness, or recalcitrant behavior. While the 20 percent exemption from the federal five-year time limit, and the somewhat stricter exemption policy in Wisconsin's new round of statewide reforms, will soften considerably the limits' impact, the question of how to respond to the most dysfunctional segment of the population is one of the unanswered dilemmas of welfare reform.

Limited Relevance

Reporters who've trumpeted Wisconsin's welfare success have based their stories on places like Fond-du-Lac or Kenosha. These successes are real—but they are of limited relevance to the nation's urban areas. The numbers in Fond-du-Lac are microscopic: sure, the caseload fell by 64 percent between January 1994 and October 1996, but in actual numbers it fell from a tiny 780 to an almost invisible 280. Moreover, the county's welfare population has a different character from inner-city populations. Fond-du-Lac has few people with no employment history and even fewer third-generation welfare recipients.

For a more realistic picture of the challenges of urban welfare reform, drive just 100 miles south of Fond-du-Lac to Milwaukee, the only industrial city in Wisconsin, where reform has had a much rockier course, one little reported in the national press. With a welfare population of 23,600—60 percent of the state's rolls—and an illegitimacy rate of 80 percent (the highest in the nation), Milwaukee has many of the same problems as Chicago, its neighbor on Lake Michigan, and New York.

Judging from the surface, you'd think Milwaukee's new programs are no different from those of Wisconsin's pioneering counties. Its four jobs centers are as clean and rationally organized as a corporate headquarters—blinking with computers, decorated in soothing mauves and pinks, and hung with cheerful cloth banners identifying the various services available to recipients. The contrast with the command center of New York City's WEP program—the battered, graffiti-bedecked Office of Employment Services—is heartbreaking. The centers offer a level of customer service unimaginable in New York: when a test-taker during a vocational assessment exam complained that the coffee was cold, the supervisor immediately called on his walkie-talkie for a new thermos.

A Different Reality

But beneath the trappings, the reality is quite different from Wisconsin's showcase counties. There, entire county administrations embrace reform and compete with one another to produce the most spectacular results. Milwaukee, by sharp contrast, suffers from fractious welfare politics. The city and county have fought Governor Thompson's reforms tooth and nail, arguing that they will increase child poverty. Local political leaders wouldn't take responsibility for the reforms, so state authorities cobbled together a consortium of 15 community service agencies to operate the new programs. Some agencies won inclusion not because of their experience or competence—which they sorely lacked—but because they lobbied successfully for a piece of the training and subsidy pie. The result is sometimes chaos. Employers find people whom they have never heard of showing up on their doorsteps expecting to work, claiming to have been referred by one of the community service agencies. Employers' calls to the agencies for assistance go unanswered. By comparison, the centralized approach of New York's workfare program looks like a model of efficiency.

Milwaukee avoids the problems of a big government jobs program, like New York's WEP, by putting workfare clients to work with nonprofit charitable organizations, such as soup kitchens or homeless shelters, or with the jobs centers themselves. But this solution has its own problems, as bad or worse than those of a government jobs program. In contrast to WEP supervisors, some of Milwaukee's nonprofits cut absentee workfare workers an enormous amount of slack, not surprising from organizations that don't usually favor tough welfare reform. And private nonprofit workfare doesn't escape the make-work problem: welfare recipients empty the trash baskets in the county's jobs centers four times a day and mechanically clean the same windows over and over again.

As agents of welfare reform, Milwaukee's nonprofits range from the satisfactory to such woefully inept examples as the job-readiness class run by YWCA employee Oralann Caldwell in one of the city's huge jobs centers. Caldwell, a tall woman with long black hair, permed bangs, and an abundance of turquoise jewelry, is trying to teach the class how to call employers about possible job openings. "Youse can put this down," she announces, writing on the blackboard: "I am a very hard and consistant [sic] worker. I have very good people skills and highly motivated [sic]." Half of the girls in the room dutifully copy the phrases; the rest slump deeper in their chairs. "Or put this down," she suggests, writing: "My nam [sic] is ____. I am a highly motivated and consistant [sic] worker with fast learning skills." She is particularly proud of this one: it combines, she says, "two pitches in one." When members of the class compose and read aloud their own pitches, Caldwell makes them worse. One bright-looking young girl suggests: "I am bilingual." Caldwell's emendation: "I have bilingual qualities."

Pessimistic Expectations

Mitchell Fromstein, chairman of Milwaukee-based Manpower, Inc., the nation's largest staffing or "temp" agency, heard this story without surprise. "It makes my stomach hurt," he responded. Fromstein has been a close observer of Milwaukee's welfare efforts, and the experience has left him pessimistic. Manpower has had a contract with the state to bring 5,000 job listings a month into the county's job center network, where welfare recipients and job seekers off the street can learn about them—this is full-employment Wisconsin, remember, where jobs go begging. Manpower did some assessments of welfare recipients' job readiness for its own information. Based on what it found, the company decided not to get further involved in Wisconsin's welfare reform effort. "I didn't want to be carried out in a stretcher," explains Fromstein.

Fromstein is an unusually authoritative judge of the challenges of welfare reform. His clients are just those businesses all welfare reform schemes expect to be the final destination of former welfare recipients. In addition, welfare reformers tout staffing agencies like Manpower as the magic solution to job placement for welfare clients, since such firms know the job market better than anyone else and have sophisticated assessment and training methods for placing people into jobs.

But what Fromstein says is troubling. "There is a big gap between the condition of the welfare population and job readiness," he concludes. Only about 40 percent of welfare recipients really want to work, he believes. Moreover, Manpower found severe limitations in welfare recipients' ability to think clearly. "Their cognitive skills are absent," says Fromstein. "Their schooling is limited, and they don't understand that at 9 A.M. the company opens and you've got to be there."

Fromstein's observations, echoed by employers across Milwaukee, point to a paradox of welfare reform: in itself, it is incapable of accomplishing its goals. Before welfare reform can succeed for a significant portion of the caseload, a far more basic revolution is necessary in the moral structure of families and communities. The cognitive deficiencies and lack of responsibility that Fromstein notes originate in miserable home environments and chaotic childhoods, years before an individual enters the workforce. No government or employer can change those conditions. . . .

The most telling statistic out of Wisconsin is this: even as the state's welfare rolls dropped precipitously, illegitimacy continued to climb. A perverse consequence of workfare, which exempts the mothers of children under a year old? Possibly. The head of the Manhattan Parks Department WEP program speculates that girls may be having lots of children now to get out of the work program, which exempts mothers with infants and toddlers. Indeed, the scariest words I heard out of Lisa McElrath's mouth were: "If I had a child, they wouldn't make me work." If we are to avoid repeating the errors of previous efforts at social betterment, people like Lisa McElrath must hear the imperative not just to work but also to behave responsibly.

CORPORATE INVOLVEMENT IN JOB-TRAINING PROGRAMS

Christina Nifong

Job-training programs can help inner-city residents find permanent employment and leave the welfare rolls, *Christian Science Monitor* reporter Christina Nifong writes in the following selection. She focuses on a successful program in Nashville, Tennessee, that began as a cooperative effort of the city leaders, the corporate headquarters of the Dollar General discount chain, and the local YMCA. As the author relates, Dollar General built a retail store in an inner-city neighborhood where poor residents could acquire the skills and experience necessary for them to move into the workforce. According to Nifong, the results of the Nashville experiment have been so positive that Dollar General has started similar programs in other cities.

The modest brick building in a forgotten neighborhood here in Nashville, Tennessee, looks beaten—its windows punched out, its walls dirtied with soot, and its roof capped with a plastic tarp.

Despite its charred facade, this shell of a Dollar General store remains an enduring symbol of hope, corporate courage, and true community grit.

It is the center of a tale of urban Tennesseans joining with a corporate partner to create one of the nation's earliest triumphs in moving inner-city residents off welfare and into jobs.

Built in the heart of a public housing project, the store has involved locals in nearly all aspects of the retail operation. The store—which sells everything from tennis shoes to laundry detergent—has become a showcase of persistence.

It appeared four years of success would be erased by arsonists in August 1997. But Nashville's poorest residents have defiantly rallied again—raising $100,000 to rebuild the store and expand the job-training program.

For American businesses, the Dollar store experience also highlights the risks and commitment required as more companies become involved in remaking the US welfare system.

"It's easy to be philosophical and global and talk about what's wrong," says Cal Turner Jr., head of the Dollar General Corp. "I'm proud of our company for saying we're going to dig in this specific instance and make a difference."

The inspiration to build a Dollar General in Nashville came during a 1992 brainstorming session in which city leaders were trying to figure out how to encourage low-income children to stay in school. They could reward them with gift certificates, they thought, perhaps provided by Dollar General. The 3,000-store discount chain is headquartered here and has set up literacy programs in 18 states.

From Concept to Reality

"And then someone said, 'Wait, there's no Dollar General store for miles around where these people live. Where would they spend their certificates?'" recalls Andrea Conte, the mayor's wife and a volunteer at a school in the public-housing neighborhood.

From that, a plan emerged to build a retail store in the Sam Levy housing complex, one of the city's most crime-ridden, and use the facility as a training ground for those on their way into the work force. They would attach a classroom to the store, where people could earn their GEDs and learn the work skills they would put into practice on-site. There, they could tackle everyday work challenges in a supportive, forgiving environment.

The project moved quickly from concept to reality. Dollar General was interested. The city's housing authority wangled a federal grant that paid for construction. In one year, store and training center were up and running.

The local YWCA was an equal partner with Dollar General in a self-sustaining arrangement, where the earnings covered the cost of paying for "interns," store stock, and learning supplies. Eventually, leaders hope any surpluses will fund community grants. In 1996, the number and nature of participants changed when the program became part of the state's welfare-reform plan. In the first 10 months of the new arrangement, 130 welfare workers found jobs.

Dollar General's Turner remembers his trepidation in the early days. He runs a publicly traded company that can't afford to have even one store be a drain on profits.

"I wanted zero publicity," he says, "because I wanted to be able to fold our tent and fade into the sunset if this failed. [Public-housing neighborhoods] are deadly locations for retailing. We knew that. I guess we were just driven by the shame of knowing that people in this neighborhood needed us."

By all accounts, the Dollar General store has been a beacon of hope in the neighborhood, and Donna Sneed's experience illustrates why. Three years ago, Ms. Sneed was in her 20s, a mother of six, and a Sam Levy resident on welfare. It took her eight months to earn her GED and complete the Dollar General-YWCA training program. Once she was out, though, her life changed dramatically. She was hired by the program to recruit other participants and teach a life-skills course. She's now off welfare and out of public housing. "People were like, if you can do it, I can too," Sneed says

Duplicating Success

The partnership was so successful that a second store-learning center was opened in Nashville. In 1996, a similar partnership began in Columbia, S.C. Other programs are in the works in Knoxville, Tenn., Mobile, Ala., and possibly St. Louis and Pittsburgh.

But progress at the original Nashville store appeared lost when it was set afire by youths in August 1997 amid anger after a white policeman killed a black man in the Sam Levy complex.

"I cried," says Sneed. "It was like everything we'd worked for had gone up in smoke. I didn't even think about rebuilding, I just thought, 'It's all done and over with.'"

But others turned their attention to rebuilding right away. Ms. Conte met with a neighborhood group the next day. They decided to raise money to rebuild at least part of the store, staging fish fries, barbecues, and bake sales if that's what it took.

They also sent two representatives to Turner in hopes of persuading him to support the effort. "I saw the feeling in those ladies," he says. "I knew that having brought hope in their community, we couldn't take it away now. I knew it would be worse to not go back than never to have gone in the first place."

With Turner's commitment, things began moving quickly. A telethon was arranged that raised $69,000 that day, with pledges for tens of thousands more. The group hoped to raise $75,000 to cover half of the cost of the inventory that was uninsured and lost in the fire. As of November 1997, they've raised more than $100,000, and expect more to come. Plans are under way to add community services with the money, such as a much-needed laundromat. Construction on the store is set to begin early in 1998.

But more than the money, the tragedy has had unexpected, positive consequences. The store created a unity of purpose within the neighborhood that has now expanded to the city at large. Groups who were unaware of the program, are now offering to help. New citywide support for the neighborhood may ease tensions with police and begin to break down racial barriers, some say.

"There are always people who want peace and want things to happen," Conte says. "But so many times that voice is drowned out by the negative ones. In this case, it wasn't. And that's very unusual."

GOVERNMENT SUPPORT OF FAITH-BASED INITIATIVES CAN HELP REDUCE POVERTY

George W. Bush

George W. Bush is the forty-third president of the United States. The following selection is taken from a speech he made to the U.S. Conference of Mayors in Detroit on June 25, 2001. Bush contends that government programs alone are not sufficient to help the poor escape poverty. Many charitable organizations run by religious groups are also doing important work to aid their impoverished neighbors, he states, but frequently these organizations do not have adequate resources to fulfill their mission. According to Bush, providing government funds to these faith-based charities will allow them to increase in size and number, therefore enabling them to help even more poor people. He maintains that such funding could be provided without violating the separation of church and state.

In 1932, one-third of Americans were unemployed. Food lines stretched for blocks. Nearly 40 percent of America's banks had failed.

Today, the story is very different. American cities are once again a magnet for ambition and culture and enterprise. The welfare rolls are down. In some places, crime rates have fallen to what they were in the mid 1960s. Problems that once seemed hopeless have yielded to reform and good sense. And the mayors of America deserve much of the credit.

Yet, as we all know, tremendous challenges still remain. Too many children, through no fault of their own, are in families without fathers and neighborhoods without opportunity. Too many young people drop out of school, drop out of the labor force and end up in prisons. Too many men and women wander alone in the twilight of addiction, illiteracy and mental illness.

New Challenges Demand New Approaches

These problems seem immune to our affluence. We're not in a post-poverty America. The challenges we face are different than they were

Excerpted from George W. Bush's remarks to the United States Conference of Mayors in Detroit, Michigan, June 25, 2001.

in the 1930s, and we must recognize new challenges demand new approaches. I realize that many of you are doing an outstanding job of dealing with these problems, and that the burden cannot fall upon you alone.

The federal government should take your side. The cities and communities of America need to be empowered, not regimented. And this is my firm commitment to you, the mayors. The agenda is long and very important. Equal opportunity is an empty hope without good schools. So the education reform legislation passed by both the House and the Senate spreads power to local communities and, for the first time, demands results in return.

It's time to act when we find that children who graduate from high school have only an 8th grade education. He's been betrayed by the adult world, and we must end that betrayal by having high expectations, strong accountability systems and the resources necessary to make sure that not one child gets left behind in America.

In the aftermath of successful welfare reform, we must turn to the problems of the working poor, especially the newly working poor. We're encouraging home ownership by providing tax credits to investors to redevelop and build new single family homes. We're facilitating home ownership for low-income families by allowing them to consolidate a year's worth of Section 8 assistance for a down payment on a home.

We believe owning something is a part of the American future. We want all people, regardless of background, to be able to claim a home of their own in America. I can't think of anything better to help revitalize the neighborhoods in America's cities. We must actively work to fill the gaps in the health care system for the working poor. That's why the budget I've sent up to Congress provides resources to expand significantly the number of community health centers, to make sure that all folks have got an opportunity for good primary care, and proposes a new tax credit for those who have difficulty affording health insurance.

Charities and Neighborhood Groups

I'm convinced that we can make progress on the important issues. Today, I want to focus on one in particular: supporting the good works of charities and neighborhood healers, empowering communities to meet their own needs and to care for their own members.

In every city, there are people who mentor and tutor; who give shelter to battered women and children; who teach biological fathers to be real and caring fathers; who help young people find jobs and avoid violence; who comfort the aged and help the dying; who picket crack houses; who walk into gunfire to end gang wars.

These good people don't lack compassion. They certainly don't lack courage. They don't lack commitment and spiritual strength. But often they lack resources. And I believe government, where it can, should stand side by side to help them.

This belief isn't owned by Republicans or Democrats. It doesn't fit into neat, ideological categories. It demands an active government to support the good works of others; an active government to spread resources and authority beyond government entirely.

In articulating his philosophy of how to aid American cities, Robert Kennedy said, there must be an overriding theme and goal: the involvement of the community, of those who have the greatest stake in the quality of the services they receive.

He spoke about putting community at the center of all our policies. He said, government back to the people of the neighborhood. I agree. In the 21st century, we should bring government back to the people who have a powerful sense of mission and idealism; back to people who know the needs of neighbors; back to people committed to rebuilding their communities from the inside out.

These committed men and women take the side of hope and compassion. And we must take their side. We must help those in need and we must encourage people to be good citizens instead of bystanders. So I'm pleased that more than 150 mayors' offices across the country are launching their own efforts to encourage faith and community initiatives in partnership with the White House.

I'm honored the U.S. Conference of Mayors has strongly endorsed my administration's faith-based and community initiative. I'm extremely proud to announce that Rosa Parks, a monumental figure in the civil rights movement, has endorsed the initiative. These are unprecedented votes of confidence. They're important steps in our efforts to bring healing and hope to those in need.

Bringing Government Back to the People

I'm excited about this approach, yet I'm under no illusions. I know government cannot be replaced by charities. The best mentoring program will never be a substitute for Medicaid for poor children. The best effort to renovate housing will never be a substitute for fair housing laws. Charities and community groups cannot do everything. But we strongly believe they can do more. We must find creative ways to expand their size and increase their number. And now is the time to start.

I proposed a new initiative to mentor the children of prisoners, so they are not further punished for the sins of their parents. I have proposed expanding federally funded afterschool programs, so that faith-based and community-based programs can access that money. I proposed a responsible fatherhood initiative, aiding community groups that seek to strengthen the role of fathers in the lives of families.

And soon, the United States House of Representatives will act on HR-7, the Community Solutions Act, sponsored by Republican J.C.

Watts and Democrat Tony Hall. The bill contains important elements of the faith-based and community initiative, and I hope you'll make your support of this legislation known to the skeptics in the United States Senate and to the United States House. HR-7 expands individual development accounts, which provide a way for charities, government and business to help struggling families find the security of assets and the dignity of independence.

The Community Solutions Act

The bill allows not-itemizing federal taxpayers to joint itemize in deducting their charitable contributions, a step that should encourage new charitable giving all across America. The Community Solution Act also expands charitable choice, the principle already established in federal law, that faith-based organizations should be able to compete for government funds without being forced to hide their religious character.

We recognize that the funds will be spent on social services, not worship services. And we recognize there must be secular alternatives for those who wish to use the services. We respect the separation of church and state, and the constitutional rights of religious people. But the days of discriminating against religious institutions simply because they are religious must come to an end if we want to heal America.

As you know, many community groups are not religious in nature. Their employees and volunteers are motivated by kind hearts and moral convictions. Yet many acts of charity and social justice are also the acts of faith. And in our cities, they are often associated with African American churches. More than 70 percent of African American churches engage in community outreach programs, including day care, job search, substance abuse prevention, food and clothing distribution. They're far more likely to apply for public funds for their social programs than other churches. And the people who most often benefit from the outreach efforts of these African American churches are poor children, who are not affiliated with any church at all.

In some places, African American churches are the only institutions that hold the fraying strands of a community together. And their work should be praised and welcomed and encouraged.

The Power of Community Action

I've heard the voices, and so have you, of the critics who are concerned about supporting good works motivated by strong faith. I suggest they go to the cities to see the need, and to see the hope. I suggest they talk to the forward-thinking mayors, mayors who are on the front line, who work closely with faith and community organizations, who are witnesses to the power of this approach.

Your witness is in Philadelphia, where Mayor John Street supports the Amachi program, directed by former Mayor Wilson Goode, which recruits mentors to care for the children of prisoners. Your witness is in Orlando, where Mayor Glenda Hood announced her faith-based and community matching grants program. That program focuses on funding youth in family projects that contribute to civic responsibility and character development.

Your witness is in Indianapolis, where my good friend, Steve Goldsmith, when he was the mayor, pioneered the Front Porch Alliance, a partnership between city hall and the values-shaping institutions in Indianapolis that helped transform this city.

You know that child care vouchers are used at houses of worship. You know the Head Start programs are often found in religious settings. You know that many public services in our cities are provided through Catholic Charities or the Salvation Army. You know that many government dollars in Medicaid and Medicare are used in religious hospitals.

In all these cases, we are funding the good works of the faithful, not faith itself. Do the critics of this approach really want to end these programs? I certainly hope not. It would be bad for America.

I understand, mayors, my administration did not invent the idea of community empowerment. But along with you, we're going to build on it. Together, we're going to convince the skeptics. Together, we're going to put the federal government and local government squarely on the side of America's armies of compassion.

There are great stories in every great city, stories of grand ambition and immigrant enterprise and cultural achievement. There are also stories of suffering, redeemed by hope and faith. And we should listen to those stories as well.

Demarco's Story

The Brightmore neighborhood in northwest Detroit can be a tough place to grow up. Some people even ask, can anything good come out of Brightmore? Well, it turns out that much good does come out of that neighborhood. At Rosedale Park Baptist Church, a group of young men and women have committed their lives to bringing hope to young African Americans.

And one of the young men they've helped is Demarco Howard. Demarco's dad had been in prison since he was a baby. His mom was addicted to drugs and was unable to raise him, so his aunt took on the responsibility and she did the very best job she could possibly do. But life was tough. Demarco was shot when he was six and spent a year in the hospital recovering. He was often in trouble, and at the age of 14, was arrested and sent to a juvenile detention facility. At that facility, Demarco met someone on the staff of Rosedale Park Baptist Church. Demarco began attending Bible study classes. And his life began to change in dramatic ways.

He goes to school, he does his homework, he goes to church, and he volunteers to help other kids in trouble. I had a chance to look Demarco in the eye and thank him for his leadership, and asked him how life was. And he said, "It's getting a lot better, Mr. President."

America can be saved, one heart, one soul, one conscience at a time. The pastor of Rosedale, Dennis Talbert, is fond of quoting a passage from the *Book of Romans*: "When I want to do good, evil is right there with me." That accurately describes the situation of many of our children in America. Evil is what his church is fighting against, with impressive results. And it's worth noting that Rosedale's outreach programs are financially supported by the Department of Justice and Michigan's Family Independence Agency, among others, and it shows what is possible.

Stories like these are being written all across America, and it's the goal of this administration to praise them at every chance, and to replicate them where we can. I hope you continue your good works as mayors. You're on the front line. At least in Washington, we don't have to worry about how the garbage gets emptied. But at least in Washington, we can work in Washington to make sure the garbage gets changed. We can make sure that we think differently about the problems that confront us. We can make sure we ask the question, "what are the results," not "what is the process." And together, we can rally the great compassion and faith and hope of America.

THE GOVERNMENT SHOULD NOT RELY ON RELIGIOUS CHARITIES TO HELP THE POOR

Polly Morrice

In the following selection, freelance writer Polly Morrice takes issue with proposals for government funding of religious charities that provide aid to the poor. Morrice argues that the government cannot support these groups without violating the constitutional policy of separating church and state. Organizations that receive federal funds must comply with antidiscrimination laws, she notes, yet many of these faith-based groups practice religious discrimination, requiring that either their members or the recipients of their services belong to a particular faith. Morrice also identifies what she feels is a larger problem: These ministries do not have a sufficient number of volunteers to cope with the expansion of their charitable responsibilities that would accompany federal funding. Many religious Americans already perform as much volunteer work as they can fit into their busy lives, she maintains, and it is unrealistic for the government to place the entire burden of solving poverty on the shoulders of these ordinary and overworked people.

Some time ago, afire with good intentions, I volunteered with a religious charity whose work I admired. I had hardly attended the orientation meeting when family circumstances forced me to resign. For years afterward, the group sent me its newsletter, which described its worthwhile projects and constant need for helping hands.

My poor showing comes to mind whenever Al Gore or George W. Bush delivers a speech on how faith-based organizations offer the last, best hope for solving the country's social problems. At first glance, the notion of shifting our burdens to such groups, through direct financing and tax credits, as Governor Bush has advocated, or through government partnerships, as both presidential candidates have suggested, has immense appeal.

After all, churches, mosques and synagogues are already battling the problems of homelessness, addiction and poverty, often successfully. At night, when public schools lock their doors, religious centers become community spaces, opening their auditoriums to Girl Scouts and Boy Scouts, to midnight basketball leagues, to A.A. [Alcoholics Anonymous] meetings. The credos of these institutions, and of their affiliated charities, stress the dignity of the people they serve. In many instances, too, their welfare programs are interfaith efforts, free of sectarian strings.

The Problems Involved

Some religious groups do, however, follow exclusionary policies, and these point up the inherent—and constitutional—difficulties of church-state partnerships. In 1999, Governor Bush toured the Haven of Rest Ministries, a homeless shelter in Akron, Ohio. In 1997, ministry officials told a Jewish businessman that he couldn't join the board, citing their rule of employing only born-again Christians.

During his visit, Mr. Bush maintained that under his plan Haven of Rest's programs would be eligible for Government funds—even though groups that accept Federal money must comply with antidiscrimination laws.

"The question we should ask," Mr. Bush said, "is 'Does it work?'" Haven of Rest Ministries, which serves 400 meals a day and lodges as many as 150 people a night, certainly meets this criterion.

Still, many Americans (and judges) resist the idea of providing public funds for groups that promote specific religious ideologies. Politicians and pundits tend to skirt the issue with a simple adjectival maneuver, recently identified by William Safire of *The New York Times:* they replace "religious" with "faith-based." Problem solved.

"Religious" has that disturbing aura of single-mindedness, while "faith-based" is comfortably vague, even cozy. Who ever heard of a "faith-based" extremist?

The Biggest Obstacle

The bugaboo of church-state separation aside, the biggest obstacle to expanding the role of religious charities may well be shortages of personnel.

When Mr. Bush pledged to "rally the armies of compassion in our communities," he was probably thinking of the millions of Americans who regularly attend worship services. Yet, far from being untested, many of these troops of the faithful are already fully engaged.

They have said yes to teaching Sunday school, buying bagels for the hospitality hour and serving on the committee for a new roof. They are leading the men's prayer circle, chauffeuring the youth group on weekly field trips, singing in the choir and coordinating the blood drive. And they have jobs, families and secular volunteer obligations to boot. To suppose that they can also complete the task of feeding and housing the nation's poor appears, at best, unrealistic.

Even the $8 billion that Mr. Bush proposes to divide among faith-based social ministries seems a bit paltry, given the magnitude of the challenges they face. Moreover, to secure the money and comply with Federal regulations, organizations would have to work with Mr. Bush's so-called Office of Faith-based Action, a new Government bureaucracy his plan would create. This agency could, conceivably, instruct Haven of Rest Ministries to drop their "born again" requirement—in which case the shelter might prefer to return the money.

As for Mr. Gore, who has endorsed a plan for Federal financing of certain types of sectarian social programs, he, too, seems convinced that battalions of spiritually motivated volunteers are thick on the ground. If you ask them, they will serve.

The truth is, the candidates—and all their fellow politicians who have lately embraced religious public service—have it partly right. An impressive number of Americans, some moved by faith and some not, make myriad, unrecompensed efforts on behalf of others.

The question is whether these ordinary people, as stressed out in their daily lives as everyone else, should be relied on by their Government to perform miracles.

A PRACTICAL ALTERNATIVE TO PUBLIC HOUSING PROJECTS

Howard Husock

The federal government developed public housing projects in an attempt to provide the urban poor with better housing than the tenements run by slumlords. However, this attempt did not succeed; the projects were rarely maintained properly and became notorious as havens of drug dealers, violent gangs, and other criminals. In the following essay, Howard Husock questions why the government feels it is necessary to provide public housing in the first place. He believes government-owned housing discourages the poor from striving to buy their own homes and undermines their incentive to maintain and improve their neighborhoods. Instead of providing public housing, the author suggests, the government should promote low-cost housing options that would increase the likelihood that poor families could buy their own homes. Husock is the director of case studies at Harvard University's Kennedy School of Government and the author of *Repairing the Ladder: Toward a New Housing Policy Paradigm*.

The U.S. public housing system seems to have embarked on a path of radical reform. Republican-sponsored legislation promises to upgrade life in the projects by changing the rules so as to attract and retain more working-class families, not just the very poor. And the Department of Housing and Urban Development plans to demolish up to 100,000 of the worst public housing units and to spend nearly $1 billion fixing up existing projects and building some 4,000 new units.

In their rush to repair and upgrade, both Congress and HUD have ignored a basic question: Why should we have a public housing system at all? Public housing, after all, was invented as an *improvement* on the private low-income housing market. That it has emerged as a major social problem in its own right would astound its promoters—and logically should suggest getting out of the business of public ownership of housing altogether. The time has come to take steps toward that end—not primarily to save money, but to allow for the emergence of a traditional alternative: strong, even if poor, neighbor-hoods based in private ownership.

Short-Term Improvements

To be sure, aspects of both the Republican and Democratic proposals are likely, at least in the short term, to improve public housing projects. The Republican plan, sponsored by Rep. Rick Lazio (R., N.Y.), would put more working and intact families in the projects (currently only 9% of tenants are married couples) and require of nonworking tenants to perform community service, which would likely make management and maintenance easier. Spending millions on improvements, as HUD plans to do, may help persuade working families to stay or even to move in, although the Clinton administration does not share Mr. Lazio's interest in raising income limits on public housing tenants.

If we must keep public housing, these steps may be helpful. But each approach raises questions. If public housing becomes a service not primarily for the very poor, why should it be a public function at all? If it is upgraded and still limited to the very poor, it is even more problematic. Why, after all, should a small minority of families gain amenities and low rent, not because they've worked hard and improved their station but because of a combination of need and luck? (Housing vouchers are no improvement over public housing in this respect.)

Given such complications, why don't we get rid of public housing? A practical answer involves the political clout of 3,400 public housing authorities scattered in congressional districts through the country. But there is also a widely held presumption that, whatever its flaws, public housing must be better than what the private market provides for poor families—demoralized places dominated by "slumlords" who charge high rents for substandard dwellings.

But it's not necessarily so—and was not so when public housing was conceived 60 years ago. Poor neighborhoods historically were places where many small-time landlords owned modest homes and rented out apartments, often living on the premises. Ownership—or the hope of it—is the surest incentive to improve and maintain one's neighborhood.

In his classic 1966 book, *The Tenement Landlord*, urban studies scholar George Sternlieb told the story of "a Negro couple in their forties. Mr. X works at the post office, his wife works at Western Electric as an assembler. The parcel [in Newark, N.J.] which they presently occupy is their second house. The first was poorer than the present one. When this present parcel is paid off, they hope to sell it and in turn move to get a better home. The rentals make it possible for them to essentially carry the house on a minimal out-of-pocket cost; and to this degree the tenement ownership is a path to upward mobility."

This traditional housing "system" can be thought of as a ladder in which different types of housing serve as individual rungs. The discipline of striving and saving to move up the ladder does more to improve the prospects of the poor than any social service program ever could. In New York City, home of the nation's largest public housing system by far, there is a celebrated new museum of the Lower East Side tenement, praised as an "urban log cabin" from which the rise of waves of immigrants began. One might just as well have a similar museum for row houses in Philadelphia, "three-deckers" in Boston or mobile homes in Phoenix.

Public housing—even if it offers physically better housing (and it has generally not been able to maintain the quality over time)—can never bring the social and individual benefits that come with individual ownership. Worse, public housing undermines ownership in poor neighborhoods by competing with private landlords for tenants. Community-development advocates talk much about the need for "asset accumulation"—that is, savings and wealth—among the poor. No publicly owned apartment, no matter how well maintained, will ever be a vehicle for that.

The proposed changes in public housing laws would demand that housing authorities act more like property managers, setting rents on each unit. They would allow mayors more control over heretofore independent local housing authorities. Each such change is contentious in its own right. But as the Congress debates such changes, it should consider them not so much in the context of improving the existing system but in another way: What approaches would best allow for a transition to private ownership?

Selling public assets to private investors is inherently complex. There would be markets for some of the better projects, or the more valuable sites. Others may have to continue in public ownership and be closed as tenants move out over time. Gradually, however, public housing and its real estate could melt into the larger housing supply. Some of its units would continue to be marketed toward poor families; some would not—just as some housing built for the middle class winds up serving the poor. Critics will charge that this will mean a loss of "affordable housing." It is shortsighted, however, to believe that the poor will only be housed if specific structures remain designated for that purpose. Cities grow and change. The poor can inherit the former homes of the middle class, as they always have. And new ways can be found to build new, modest housing for those of modest means.

A New Role

If HUD got out of the business of owning and managing properties, it could find a new role helping stimulate research into new, low-cost housing forms and suggesting ways in which local jurisdictions can change regulations so as to permit the least expensive, but still safe, housing to be built. (Miami officials, for instance, are considering changing codes that demand expensive hurricane-proofing, because new, inexpensive "quick-crete" concrete can do the job at lower cost.)

Advances in manufactured housing offer the prospect that new technologies can do for the price of housing what Wal-Mart, Kmart and their suppliers have done for the price of clothing. HUD could also assist cities in assembling sites and cleaning up "brownfields" [land that has been polluted by industry and then abandoned] in older urban areas, so as to permit the construction of new, low-cost neighborhoods to serve the lower ends of the housing market. In short, it's time to end a housing policy based on the belief that markets can't deliver shelter to those of modest means—and time to recognize that markets bring with them a social structure that the best-intentioned public ownership can never match.

PROVIDING BETTER HOUSING FOR THE POOR

Alexander von Hoffman

Alexander von Hoffman is a fellow at the Joint Center for Housing Studies at Harvard University's Kennedy School of Government and the author of *Local Attachments: The Making of an American Neighborhood, 1850–1920*. In the following selection, he describes the grassroots campaign to build low- and moderate-income housing in cities across the United States, which is transforming blighted neighborhoods into desirable places to live. Von Hoffman explains that after the federal government slashed funding for subsidized housing in inner-city neighborhoods during the 1980s, community-development corporations and nonprofit organizations stepped in to fill the gap. These groups build between twenty-thousand and forty-thousand homes annually for poor Americans, the author notes, as many as the federal government averaged during its peak years of providing subsidized housing. Moreover, he writes, these organizations stress the importance of including the low-income residents in the process, which boosts their sense of community and encourages self-improvement.

In 1983 the makers of *The Day After*, a made-for-television movie about the aftermath of a nuclear holocaust, filmed part of their drama in an inner-city neighborhood in Kansas City whose forlorn, rubble-strewn landscape seemed the perfect image of a fictional ground zero. Today that same site is a development that includes 300 units of low- and moderate-income housing, three shopping centers, and a library. No new government program brought about this remarkable transformation; rather, a private local nonprofit organization, the Community Development Corporation of Kansas City, took the initiative.

The revival of this once-forsaken piece of Kansas City real estate is part of a little-celebrated but widespread campaign by community and nonprofit organizations to build low-income housing and revitalize inner-city neighborhoods across the United States. Unlike conventional government housing programs, the new housing movement is based in the communities it seeks to help, relies as much on private as on public funding, and produces homes that could be mistaken for upscale condos. It aims to engage the poor in improving their own lives. In an era of hostility to government the community-based approach to housing has wide political appeal. Along with Senator Carol Moseley-Braun, of Illinois, and other liberal Democrats, such staunch Republicans as Senator Kit Bond, of Missouri; Congressman Rick Lazio, of New York; and even Governor Kirk Fordice, of Mississippi, a rock-ribbed Reagan conservative, have publicly endorsed the community-based housing movement. Yet, strangely, it has eluded public awareness. It is making a visible impact on low-income neighborhoods all over the country, but the question remains whether it can survive, much less conquer the monumental problems of the inner city.

The Movement's Origins

The movement originated in the 1960s but first took root in the 1970s, when job and population flight, disinvestment, arson, drugs, crime, and disease were ravaging many urban neighborhoods. As these destructive forces spread to large urban public-housing projects, Charles Murray and other conservatives concluded that government social programs had actually caused the chaos. In the early 1980s the federal government, under President Ronald Reagan, began slashing the funds available for subsidized housing.

Today the federal government has all but ceased to build low-income housing, and in 1996 President Bill Clinton signed a bill that stopped granting rent subsidies to new applicants. Meanwhile, rising housing costs take ever larger bites of the limited wages of the working poor: by 1993 one-fifth of the nation's unsubsidized renters paid half or more of their income for shelter. In this grim context new initiatives in the housing field have become crucial.

In response to the federal retreat from housing, groups of private citizens set out to create islands of safety and comfort in some of the toughest slums in the country. There are now about 4,000 local housing organizations in the United States. Since 1988 they have developed more than 20,000 homes a year for low-income Americans. In 1994 community-based groups built approximately 40,000 units—equivalent to the rates of production achieved by the government during the heyday of public housing.

Community-Development Corporations

The organizations that produce and manage low-income housing differ markedly from the rigid centralized bureaucracies that run most government housing programs. Community-development corporations, which are chartered nonprofit associations, figure prominently among the producers of low-income housing. CDCs were first created in the 1960s, to encourage business activity in inner-city ghettos, but the vast majority concentrate on housing.

Unlike public housing, community-based housing exists in the private market; its developers must at least break even in order to survive and carry out their ambitious agendas. Thus they seek both public and private sources of funding. In collaborative meetings—or, occasionally, in dramatic confrontations—local housing groups wheedle loans, grants, and free land and utilities from city, state, and federal officials.

The Intermediaries

Special kinds of nonprofit organizations, known as intermediaries, raise private funds and funnel them to hundreds of local housing and community developers across the United States. By acting as a combination of broker, credit-rating service, and rich uncle, two large intermediaries have emerged as powerhouses in the movement. The Local Initiatives Support Corporation, or LISC, was started by the Ford Foundation as a permanent institution for helping distressed neighborhoods. James Rouse's Enterprise Foundation, one of the foremost national housing organizations, founded by the head of the Rouse Company, an innovative development company, was designed to give the housing movement economy of scale. Each organization maintains a national headquarters and multiple branch offices and raises millions of dollars each year from foundations and corporate donors. (Also, the Neighborhood Reinvestment Corporation, created by Congress as a public nonprofit corporation, maintains an extensive network of local housing organizations.)

Both LISC and Enterprise create pools of housing-project deals that they offer to philanthropists and investors; the intermediaries then monitor the community groups responsible for the projects to ensure that they perform as promised. One reason that LISC and Enterprise can persuade businesses to provide capital to small community organizations is that low-income housing is, generally, profitable. With the help of tax benefits, especially the Federal Low Income Housing Tax Credit (which housing developers earn and then sell to investors), investments yield an average annual return of about 16 percent over fifteen years. Attracted by such earnings, hard-nosed business investors, including Warren Buffett, the celebrated financier, have plunged into housing for the poor.

Some critics dislike all the high finance and charge that community-based housing is simply a money racket. Old-style champions of public housing and direct housing subsidies object to the syndication of tax credits and other development deals, because the transaction costs benefit lawyers and accountants. Yet in a climate of government reductions and budget cutbacks a housing system under the direct control of public or semi-public agencies is simply not a viable alternative. The days of well-funded centralized programs are not about to return anytime soon.

In fact the combination of self-sufficiency, good management, local control, and profitability gives the private-public approach to low-income housing a powerful political appeal that government housing programs never had. Wooed by LISC and Enterprise, executives of the Weyerhaeuser Company, Hallmark Cards, Bank of America, and other corporations have become ardent supporters of the housing movement.

Builders of Low-Income Housing

The best-known nonprofit housing organization is Habitat for Humanity. Founded by Millard Fuller, a devout former businessman, in 1976, to witness the Christian gospel by building simple but adequate housing for the poor, and often associated with Jimmy Carter, who is probably its most famous supporter, Habitat organizes volunteers to help low-income people literally build houses for themselves. Critics dismiss Habitat as insignificant, on the grounds that its local chapters are highly decentralized and build only a few houses at a time. But it has some 1,300 local chapters in the United States, and volunteer work on Habitat projects is increasingly popular, especially among Protestant congregations. Thus Habitat for Humanity regularly ranks as one of the largest homebuilders in the United States.

Habitat is national—indeed, international—in scope, but regional housing organizations, working on their own or with community groups, also develop impressive amounts of low-income housing. Started in Boston at the dawn of the housing movement, The Community Builders has in the past thirty-three years developed more than 8,300 units of low- and moderate-income housing. It currently manages 4,445 units in the northeastern United States, and has about 4,000 more units on the way. In the San Francisco Bay area BRIDGE Housing Corporation has helped to produce about 7,000 units throughout California over the past thirteen years. The New York City Housing Partnership, founded in 1982 by David Rockefeller, has worked with private capital and the state and city governments to build 13,000 new homes in fifty low-income communities throughout the five boroughs of New York City.

The movement has drawn in organizations whose original purpose was other than housing. In the sprawling inner-city district made famous by the Rodney King riots, Concerned Citizens of South Central Los Angeles was started in 1985 to fight the construction of a giant waste incinerator, but it has since developed and now manages more than a hundred units of low-income housing. The primary and still radical goal of the Industrial Areas Foundation, founded by the late Saul Alinsky, is to organize disenfranchised people so that they can seize power for themselves; yet the powerful coalitions of church and community organizations that the IAF has launched also build homes for low-income citizens in cities such as New York and Baltimore.

Even commercial firms, albeit socially committed ones, build low-income housing: McCormack Baron & Associates, of St. Louis, a leader among for-profit residential builders in urban areas, works on large-scale redevelopment projects across the country. Telesis Corporation, of Washington, D.C., is administering court-ordered low-income housing developments in Dallas and Yonkers among its other projects.

Two Rules for New Housing

Two ironclad rules influence the appearance of the new housing. First, the architecture must not look anything like the uniform barracks and high-rise slabs of conventional public-housing projects. Second, the buildings must be well maintained: managers take pride in making quick repairs, and no graffiti are allowed to mar the walls. Several of the housing groups hire neighborhood youths as guards and maintenance men to ensure that their property is not vandalized.

Although cost constraints and the desire to make low-income housing look inconspicuous give many projects a bland appearance, architects have also produced stylish buildings that could easily be mistaken for upmarket residential developments. David Baker has designed two striking low- and moderate-income condominium projects in San Francisco for BRIDGE: Parkview Commons, hillside apartments with Mediterranean clay-tile roofs; and Holloway Terrace, two-story houses with sculptured white-stucco walls. Working in Boston, Goody, Clancy & Associates used traditional Boston brick and tall bay windows to make Langham Court, a mixed-income project, fit into the Victorian South End neighborhood.

Perhaps the best-known architect specializing in low-income housing is Michael Pyatok, of Oakland, California, who despite small budgets manages to create comfortable living spaces, safe and inviting interior courts, and attractive exteriors composed of bays and trellises. His work ranges from James Lee Court, an apartment block with earth-colored stucco walls decorated with colorful African patterns, which houses twenty-six formerly homeless families in Oakland, to what he mockingly calls a "Ralph Lauren–style" suburban development for mixed incomes in Bellevue, Washington, which looks for all the world like an exclusive subdivision.

Always struggling with zoning restrictions and the fears of suburbanites, Pyatok has learned to be clever. In the face of a requirement that each unit have two parking spaces (although the families could afford one car at most), Pyatok persuaded a zoning board to allow the extra parking spaces to be used as a basketball court. To lend a reassuring single-family image to a low-income multi-family project, he resorted to picket fences, individual entries, and chimney-like cupolas that hid telltale bunches of ventilation pipes.

Low-Income Homes

Neighbors aside, the primary goal is to give poor people themselves a sense of pride and a stake in the community. To do so, many housing groups promote homeownership. In Michigan, for example, Kalamazoo Neighborhood Housing Services coordinates second-mortgage lending programs with down payments as low as $1,000, offers home-rehabilitation loans, and gives classes to first-time homeowners in budgeting and repairs.

Other groups, among them The Resurrection Project, in the Pilsen neighborhood of Chicago, build and sell one- and two-family houses. Suburban ranch houses have begun to appear in low-income urban neighborhoods, thanks to Habitat for Humanity, which builds a basic version, and to the Mid-Bronx Desperadoes (officially, MBD Community Housing Corporation), which sponsored the construction of classic ranches on Charlotte Street, where both Jimmy Carter and Ronald Reagan stopped to view the desolation of the South Bronx.

Most housing groups build and sell only a few houses at a time, but East Brooklyn Congregations, a federation of churches organized by the Industrial Areas Foundation, has taken a radically different approach. It pioneered the Nehemiah Plan in the East New York and Brownsville sections of Brooklyn. Named by Johnny Ray Youngblood, a Brooklyn minister, after the Old Testament prophet who rebuilt Jerusalem, the Nehemiah Plan aims to construct and sell very inexpensive homes en masse to the working poor, thus literally building an entire community of homeowners. Since 1982 East Brooklyn Congregations has constructed and sold about 2,150 two-story single-family row houses; another 1,250 are in the works.

As a result, an urban Levittown now flourishes in what was one of the poorest and most troubled parts of New York City. The homeowners—church members, former public-housing tenants, and longtime neighborhood residents—scrupulously maintain their property. A visitor cannot help being struck by the contrast between the Nehemiah houses—whose owners have adorned them with doves, lions, and other front-gate statuary, manicured front lawns, and rooftop satellite dishes—and the anonymous graffiti-scarred high-rise public-housing projects in an adjoining district.

Some housing advocates slight the Nehemiah Plan for taking a no-frills approach and creating a low population density in an urban area, but the real-estate market reflects the popular judgment on the plan and its neighborhoods: row houses that originally sold for $39,000 to $62,000 are now valued at $125,000.

Despite their different approaches, the developers of low-income housing share certain basic assumptions. They fervently believe that their organizations must be run as competent business enterprises, that their housing developments should encourage self-sufficiency and self-improvement among the low-income residents, and that local control is the key to their success.

Still, despite this record of success, the question remains whether the movement can do more than make a dent in a daunting problem. Skeptics scoff at the notion that it can solve the rampant problems of the inner city any more than the government's War on Poverty could during the 1960s. Even people within the movement complain that some narrowly focused or poorly organized CDCs take years to build a few units of housing and then do little else. The funding process is complex and time-consuming: whereas commercial developers generally obtain financing from one or two lenders, community-based developers may need the participation of a dozen sources, each with different criteria for approval. And because of its grassroots nature, the movement has spread unevenly. It has yet to reach some smaller cities and parts of the South and Midwest.

People at LISC and Enterprise have responded by training community leaders in management and planning in order to "build capacity" in local organizations. There are signs of progress: the number of housing groups that have each produced more than a hundred units is climbing. If funders would adopt uniform application forms for loans and grants, the housing movement could streamline funding. Above all, housing advocates must protect the Low Income Housing Tax Credit, federal block grants, and other financial sources, which are the lifeblood of so many housing developments.

Neighborhoods Ripe for Redevelopment

Pessimists overlook the role that community-based housing groups can play in helping to revive inner-city neighborhoods as stable working-class districts. Having lost population and buildings, inner-city neighborhoods are ripe for redevelopment. Left to themselves, they will continue to deteriorate or else gentrify as real-estate developers move in to make a killing. However, upwardly mobile African-Americans and immigrants who live in or adjacent to depressed neighborhoods contribute stability and economic resources to the inner city. Most important, the movement is able to tap the strong desire of many poor people to overcome the problems of poverty and improve their lot in life. Wherever it has advanced, the sense of hope and optimism is almost palpable.

In the South Bronx, once an international symbol of urban crime and devastation, a concerted rebuilding campaign by dozens of housing and community groups and the city government has created vital neighborhoods completely at odds with images of despair. On 165th Street stands a grand old apartment building renovated by the Morrisania Revitalization Corporation and renamed Jacquline Denise Davis Court. Today it houses people with very low incomes; about a third of the residents were homeless prior to moving in.

Despite their poverty, the occupants of this building are engaged in community life as never before. The tenant association runs its own building patrol and, from a table in the brightly restored foyer, checks everyone who enters the front door. The tenants hold bake sales and throw building parties on holidays. They organized a successful phone-and-mail campaign to persuade the transit authority to restore bus service in front of the building after a ten-year hiatus.

Places like Jacquline Denise Davis Court are sprouting up all over the country. Although often unheralded, these small triumphs are the most powerful argument for community-based housing. There is new life at the ground zeroes of urban America.

CHAPTER 4

LIFE IN THE INNER CITY: PERSONAL ACCOUNTS

Contemporary Issues
Companion

LIVING IN FEAR

Earl Shorris

In inner-city neighborhoods, poverty and drugs transform the role of neighbors from friends who can be counted on in times of trouble to strangers who are feared and cannot be trusted. In the following excerpt from his book *New American Blues: A Journey Through Poverty to Democracy*, Earl Shorris illustrates this situation through an account of the experiences of Lucia Medina, a young woman living in an impoverished neighborhood in Chicago. Medina describes a time in her life when she and her family lived in a residential hotel filled with junkies and thieves. Her belongings were stolen so often, she relates, that she began to take her most valued possessions with her whenever she left her room. Although she was finally able to move into an apartment, Medina says that she still fears her neighbors, and it is not unusual for her children to hear gunfire in the streets.

In old movies and novels now mostly forgotten the poor know hunger and sometimes cold, but they do not know loneliness. In the 24th Ward of Chicago at the end of the depression and in the early 1940s, when poverty seemed absolute, life flowed from one family to another, reached beyond the walls of any house, into the streets, across the back porches; a neighborhood in that time was the name of a collection of neighbors. Nothing like a neighborhood exists in a world of relative poverty. Snitches live in the housing projects, a woman visits another in the afternoon to sell a little dope, no one can be trusted; the children are always in danger.

The Role of Neighbors

Poverty changes the role of neighbors. The game of modern society converts them from allies to adversaries; they become a force, equals against each other, violent or threatening violence, lurking, bound to the rules of the game. The poor do not live in the comfort of neighbors, but in fear of them. Someone or something bad, dangerous, lives next door to the poor; they must always be ready to deal with it. To let down one's guard, in a moment of trust or a sigh of weariness, invites disaster.

This conversion, from a city of neighbors to a world of adversaries, perhaps more than any other single factor, affects the ability of the poor to break out of [poverty].

Lucia Medina's Story

When I first met Lucia Medina, she was still obese. Since then, she has lost over a hundred pounds, and in the last year or so a beautiful young woman in her early thirties has begun to emerge from the blurred flesh. When she smiles, deep dimples occur in both cheeks. Her skin is as smooth as that of her five-year-old daughter and it is the color of milk touched by coffee. In her apartment, on a computer so old that its contents cannot be extracted but lie inside as still as if they were carved in stone, she has written the first chapters of a novel. "A romance," she said, "a fantasy romance," and laughed.

No one in Lucia Medina's family, in all the history that can be remembered, has ever been anything but poor. They have lived for generations, perhaps centuries, in the surround. She uses other words to describe her situation, but there can be no doubt that it is the surround. "It's like you're contained," she said of life among her neighbors in the projects and the hotels. "You can't go out, let your kids to play or anything, because you're always worried: Who's out there?

"I don't think you ever get over it. When you look at it, you might put it in the back of your head, but I don't think you ever get over it."

She began as an equal despite her history, a pretty girl and a straight A student until she had a miscarriage, followed by dangerous hemorrhaging. Her teachers told their straight A student that she had spent so much time in the hospital that she would have to repeat the year. With the stubborn sense of honor that deflects the lives of Latinos, especially the poor, she dropped out of school rather than repeat the year.

She lived with a man for eight years before she married him. "And it still turned out bad," she said. "After we got married, he got possessive. Everybody had to go like under his command: You're my wife and you have to do this and you have to do that. And if I didn't do it, he would get upset and he would go out drinking with his friends."

They separated, got together again, lost their bearings in the city. "We wound up in a hotel," she said, "the whole family, me and the kids and my husband, because we couldn't find a place. It was hard. We were in the Prince George, a lot of different ones. And then the places they put you in, you'd rather sleep in the street than in the hotel. It's drab, there's dealers and prostitutes and you name it, they got it. We had one room. It was about the size of my dining area. We had bunk beds. There was two bunk beds here, two bunk beds there, then the baby in the crib. A little chair, a little table. And then they steal everything you have. Everything I owned they stole, the people who have passkeys. They watch you and somebody else steals your stuff. You complain. You go to the cops, and they can't do much. I tried.

"When someone knocks at the door, I open it a little and show them a knife, a big knife. I think if I had to protect myself or my kids, I would use it. At night, because I'm scared, I sleep with the knife under my pillow and I push the dresser and the chest up against the door so I'll hear it move if they try to get in."

Dealing with Child Welfare

About that time, her oldest daughter, Yvette, a plump child with heavy eyebrows and dark skin, brown painted over gray, decided that she was white. No matter what her parents said, Yvette could not be dissuaded from her new image of herself. She was a difficult child, headstrong, beginning to show signs of something strange. Her father responded angrily. He "hit her on the butt," according to Mrs. Medina. In school the next day Yvette told her teacher that her father had punched her in the stomach and beat her with a belt buckle.

The teacher called the Child Welfare Agency (CWA), who put Yvette in a foster home. Then Mrs. Medina was told to bring the other children in to be examined. It was merely a demonstration of good faith, the child welfare worker said. If there was nothing wrong, she would be allowed to take the children home. But there was no good faith on the part of the CWA. "They kept them," Mrs. Medina said. "My other children were fine, and they went into the system also, because we were living in a hotel, and they considered anybody who was in a hotel bad. The system is in charge of your life. It gets to that point. They do things. Your life is worth nothing. They own you. You're just a number."

After that, she entered into a half-crazed routine, up all night in the hotel, fearing that at any moment she would hear the dresser pushed away from the door as someone entered their room, and "All day I kept trying to get the kids back, going to the child bureau agency, and to find out why it happened.

"There was not enough to live on, you live on cold cuts. We used to pick up cans. It helps a little bit. There was a time when I carried my hotplate with me, because that was the most valuable thing to me at that time. They can't take your spoons and forks and pots, but the hotplate they could sell it on [to another person]. I had a little one and I carried it with me everywhere. And then I would buy whatever I needed that day, come down here [to the Lower East Side where she was raised], walking, where the food is cheaper, and take it with me.

An Inside Job

"I used to make stew, steak. With a little oil, you fry it. Soups. But you only buy so much. You have a little refrigerator, but then if you buy meat, they're gonna take your meat. There was a lock. When we would come back it was still locked. They had a key. That's what you call an inside job.

"It's like you got your back against the wall and let em all throw stuff at you.

"Then somebody from the hotel asked my husband if he wanted protection or whatever, join them and they won't be stealing our stuff no more and he would be getting money or whatever. He thought about it, but I wouldn't have it.

"After being hungry and eating sandwiches for months, he said, 'Yeah! You know, it's money to eat. You won't have to be eating sandwiches every day. You could go to the restaurant to eat a steak once in a while.'

"When you're hungry, you think that's like gold, but I wouldn't have it. He was upset. He would get loud. Can't do nothing else but get loud. I told him it's not worth it in the long run, it causes more problems.

"They just asked him once, because they kept stealing from us, stealing our hotplates, and stealing our food and everything we had."

More Problems

In the end, her moral stance made no difference. "He went to jail," she said. "He took a loan or something, and they said he stole the money when we were in the hotel. He took a loan of money, and I don't know. He didn't tell me. And the person had said he took the money from them. Somebody in the hotel. There were loan sharks. He was sent for a year. It was the first time he had been in jail.

"I just had Monica [her youngest child]. She was an infant, and I was trying to protect her so they wouldn't put her in foster care, so I was like on the run all the time. Then I'm carrying my hotplate, carrying my daughter in the pouch and going to different hotels."

When at last she was able to arrange to move into an apartment rented by her aged uncle, the Child Welfare Agency returned her children to her. The oldest girl, Yvette, had been molested while she was in the foster home. The boy, Jeremy, was in worse condition. "My son was two and a half and he only weighed twenty pounds," she said. "And they had told me he was gonna be crippled, he wasn't gonna be able to speak or hear anything, because he was really bad. He kept bleeding from his nose. I think they were hitting him. He wasn't getting the food, the nutrients that he needed to get."

While she was in foster care, Yvette began to have seizures. By the age of thirteen, she had been diagnosed as epileptic, asthmatic, and schizophrenic. There is no doubt that she is a difficult child, sometimes unmanageable, biting, and threatening to kill her mother, but whenever I saw her, which was only three or four times, she was neat and cheerful. Once, when we went to the store together to buy doughnuts and coffee, she talked about her love of mathematics. She is a big girl for her age, and at times her dark eyes and heavy eyebrows have the intensity of a Frida Kahlo portrait.

By 1994, they had settled in with Mrs. Medina's uncle, who had an apartment on the first floor of a project on the Loisaida [A pun used by people of Puerto Rican descent. Loíza is a river in Puerto Rico named after a princess. The district called the Loisaida is known formally as the Lower East Side.]. The family does not know the neighbors there, except to fear and despise them. They gather in the hallway outside the apartment, shouting and banging against the door, big men, threatening, and children out of control, while the women pass through the gauntlet carrying bundles or dragging children by the hand.

Instead of a dresser, Lucia Medina has a huge iron plate braced against the door. Whenever the door is opened, the iron plate must be pulled aside and dropped to the floor. The clang of the iron against the concrete floor reverberates through the apartment, stopping conversation, laughter, crying, even movement.

Once, in winter, when a sudden warm spell came over the city, all the flies hatched early and filled the apartment. Every night, outside their windows, garbage piles up on the grass. It is the work of their neighbors. The Medinas keep cats in defense. At evening, the children see the rats scurrying through the trash that piles up on the little plot of grass between the project and the sidewalk. They ask about them. They ask about drug dealers, numbers runners, gunfire in the streets.

Lucia Medina said that when she was a girl, she liked to draw and write poems. "I like Elizabeth Browning," she said.

"Even now?"

She nodded.

Dreams

On afternoons when she and the children and I talked while her uncle traveled about the apartment on his electrically powered wheelchair or when we met over a lunch of *mofongo* or *pernil* at a little restaurant called Adela's, she sometimes dreamed aloud: "I was thinking of going to Arizona. I would like to go to California. I would like to go into a different scenery to see how it goes. It's far away. I like Arizona, because I hear the air is dry. I've seen pictures. A lot of stuff they show on the History on TV about the Indians and stuff is beautiful."

When she spoke so, she often looked away, not to a window but to a corner of the room near the ceiling, as if infinity were there. She dreamed only of places she had never seen and of people who had long since died into history.

THE RESPONSIBILITIES OF AN INNER-CITY GRANDMOTHER

Betty Washington, as told to Elijah Anderson

Elijah Anderson is the author of *Code of the Street: Decency, Violence, and the Moral Life of the Inner City.* In the following selection from his book, Anderson presents the narrative of a Philadelphia resident whom he refers to by the pseudonym of Betty Washington. A forty-year-old divorced woman, Washington explains that she is raising the children of her drug-addicted daughter. Rather than see her grandchildren taken to foster homes, Washington quit her job and went onto welfare so that she could care for them full time. As much as she loves and enjoys her grandchildren, she acknowledges that she has taken on a difficult responsibility, especially since the children have health and developmental problems due to their mother's drug use during her pregnancies.

I'll be forty in August, and I was born here in Philadelphia, North Philly. When the drugs came in around the corner, everything just went crazy, you know, completely crazy. And even though I lost my house in a fire, I wouldn't want to go back there either. It was really bad there. My oldest daughter, that's where she really had her problems at. It was a mixed neighborhood, Puerto Rican. When I had my first daughter, I was eighteen. I have two girls. One will be twenty-one in July, and the oldest one's just turned twenty-two. . . .

When I got pregnant with my first daughter, I was married. I had both my children while I was married, but I haven't been married twenty years. I got divorced. . . .

Trying to Raise Children Alone

I raised my daughters on my own pretty much, with the help of my mom. It was not a problem until they got older 'cause she was so attached to them. There was a lot of problems there. I had a boyfriend. That didn't work out either. We had a lot of problems raising Angela. It's hard raising a child and you get a mother interferin', you know. We were younger then. I say she was younger too and set in her ways. So when I started having problems with my daughters, she couldn't see it, because she wasn't there every day, you know, and then after everything came to a head and everything got out of hand, she took 'em. *Then* she was able to see what I was talkin' about.

They would run away a lot. They were twelve and eleven. After we had the fire, it was real emotional. I was tryin' to get everything situated with the insurance. I had a lot of problems, you know. I got ripped off with my insurance and the contractors and everything. The house never did get fixed up. And things just wasn't as they were. I hadda go out and work. I had to start doin' things that they wasn't used to. They was used to bein' with me, and then I had to start goin' out findin' a job, lookin' for a job, leavin' them with different people. And it just caused a lot of problems with them, and they couldn't adjust. Sometimes they would stay at home, sometimes they'd stay with a neighbor, sometimes they'd stay with my mom. At the time when they really needed me, I couldn't really be there for them. So it was hard. Goin' back to the district attorney, goin' back to the court. It was difficult.

And their whole behavior just changed. Angela was twelve years old. She started doin' drugs. Well, at the time it was marijuana. It was the neighborhood. They got kind of wild. They were gettin' more freedom, much more freedom. There was a lot of peer pressure. She used to start doin' things that were so out of place for her. And I guess I was a little strict on her, you know, on account of it was just me. I had to be the mother and the father. And once I started lettin' 'em get out there, they just changed. Well, she has always been a bad, problem child. She got kicked out of first grade. And then the neighborhood started deterioratin' and there was a lot of peer pressure, and she's not the type of person that could stand on her own. She listens to everybody on the outside, no matter what you say. . . .

A Bad Seed

I know I brought her up right; I know I did everything right for her. I might not have been *the best,* 'cause I had problems myself. I couldn't do everything, but I did the best I could, but she's—I don't know— she's just a bad seed. My other daughter was a A student. She was one of the first kids they took out of the regular public school and sent to white neighborhoods, takin' the bus. She was good. But then she got on drugs. She was supposed to go to the School for the Performing Arts. She could have went to Cheyney College. She could have done anything she wanted.

But Angela, she just a bad child. She didn't care what you do to her if you punish her, how much you talk to her, how much you cry, scream, whatever. She didn't care. Like I say, to me it was a lot of peer pressure. A lot of what she did had to do with bein' that we were livin' in a Puerto Rican neighborhood. Most of the problems I had were with Puerto Rican guys. I had to go out to these people and fight 'em: "Leave my daughter alone." She almost got shot by the cops 'cause she was livin' around the corner in an abandoned house with a whole bunch of those guys. And it was a shock too because I didn't think that she was socializin' with them. The way I had brought her up, it was out of place, completely out of place. The first time I actually had to leave my job and come home because she had ran away was because of marijuana. She was just stoned. She was doin' weird stuff. First I thought it was attention; she wanted a lot of attention. But she really had a problem.

It came to it that she had to be put away. I had to actually put her in a home, and I regret the day I did that because instead of her gettin' better, everything got worse in there. It just got worse. But at the time there was nothin' else I could do. I had myself to think about. I had the youngest one to think about. And this child, she wanted to fight. She pulled knives on me, she said people were gonna blow the house up. This is the type of child that she was. I got her back after about a year. She was doin' the same thing, still wantin' to fight and whatnot. And I didn't think that DHS [Department of Human Services] was really helpin' as much as they could have been.

When she went on crack, her whole attitude changed: "I just don't give a damn" attitude. And she was so—how can I say it?—she had no scruples about it, none whatsoever. After I got her back—she was nineteen—she stayed here for a while, but at the time I didn't really, really notice she was doin' crack. I knew she smoked marijuana. We started goin' to the same school. I was goin' for the computers, and she was goin' for nurse's aide. And she did good, A's and whatnot, but she didn't complete it. And I still didn't really know, because at the time she was staying with my mother again and she was back and forth here. And she got pregnant. And she as always startin' fightin', and I couldn't deal with that, so I had to put her out while she was pregnant. The landlord's daughter lives upstairs. That caused a lot of problems 'cause the landlord would find out what was goin' on. She wanted to bring boys in, she didn't want to do nothin', she wanted to fight all the time, so I had to ask her to leave. And I really didn't connect it to the crack. I knew she was doin' somethin', but I just didn't know she was doin' that. And then after she had the baby, I still didn't know. They didn't really tell me too much. She didn't stay in the hospital too long. I was thinkin' they let her go, but actually she left the hospital.

Betty Becomes a Grandmother

Then that's when she said, "You're still my momma." I stayed over with her for a week, and she would go out, and she would not come back. Eventually, she went fourteen days and she didn't come back, so I wound up bringin' the baby back here with me. And that's when I realized she was on the crack. She was not behavin' like a mother. But she's always been the type of person who eventually lets you know what she's doin'. And she come home, she told me she was doin' what not. And by then I had already knew. By me takin' the baby back to the clinic and everythin', the doctors told me. I didn't understand what was goin' on with the baby, the withdrawal symptoms and what not. I had already made up my mind, if she wasn't goin' to take care of the baby, if she wasn't goin' to do right, then I would take him. But I tried to give her a chance to take care of her own baby, but that didn't work out. I had to stay here. She wasn't ever here. Jamaicans would come lookin' for her wantin' me to give 'em back their money that she took. I'd give her money to go get Pampers and milk, and she'd take that. I sent her to the Laundromat. Someone else would bring the clothes back, she's gone with the money.

What I did was I went with her to court because she knew I was goin' to find out eventually. She went to get custody of her baby, but she didn't have any place to stay. And the address she used, she couldn't stay there, because these people was involved in drugs, you know. And we got joint custody. I figured when we had joint custody, everything would work out. That didn't work out. So I had to get full custody. By the time he was ten months, I had full custody. . . .

Now I have the little baby. She's thirteen months now. I got custody of the oldest boy. I went to court. That's a lot of money goin' back and forth to court. You know, I had to do that; then the father, he decided he wants to get upset because I won't let him see them when he wants to see them. You know, he had a set time to come and see 'em. He never showed up, but he took me to court. I had to wind up payin' the money, altogether about seven hundred dollars, and still to this day we have four court orders for him to come and see his son on Sunday from one to three; he has not once showed up, not once, not one time.

Crack Baby

When you have a crack baby, it's always some problem. It can be physical. You don't really understand the babies, what the babies want from you, you know, the crying, the anger. The babies get hyper, you know, they get really upset, and that's a lot to deal with, a lot to deal with. So you take them back and forth to the clinic. And there's always somethin' wrong with these children. What really happened with this baby, the little boy, he wound up with some kind of infection. I knew she [Angela] had herpes, but I didn't know she had syphilis. The baby got sick, and they thought he had meningitis. Well, if I didn't have custody of him, there was no way that I could have had him treated without the mother. Where was I supposed to find her at? Where was I supposed to look for her at? And I didn't know at the time, but I found out two months later she had syphilis, second stage, secondary syphilis. And that's hard, that's really hard.

She fades in and out of my life. If she's not at the hospital right now, I couldn't tell you where she is. She just had another baby, only weighed two pounds, it's still in the hospital. Right now, the little baby, I'm trying to get custody of her. I filed a petition to get custody of her. What they're telling me now is you've got to have an address for the father and the mother. I don't have the address. I don't know where they are. They say I have to go find 'em. Where am I supposed to look for them at? I know nothin' about the father. I don't know where to find the mother unless she's in the hospital. She might be there two days; then she's gone. To get custody of her, you have to get involved with DHS. It's so different from last year because once she got tested for cocaine and they knew she didn't have a place to stay, the baby was automatically turned over to DHS. All she had to do was agree to let me have her, which she did. Like I say, I have her now for thirteen months. The new baby, I don't know what they're goin' to do with, I really don't. She still don't have a place to stay. She still test cocaine. What the social worker tells me now is "Just because she's doin' cocaine doesn't mean you can take the baby from her," which is so different from last year, you know.

From the World of Work to the World of Welfare

But you have to step in and take the responsibility. You have no other choice. I don't want to see him in a foster home, and I would hate to see right now for them to be split up like that. But it's hard. Yeah, everything is in God's hands. He show you what you have to do and what you don't have to do. The only problem I have is that there's no man in my life. I don't have time for those things no more. Everything is those children. Everything is a circle around those kids. You have to have a place to stay, you have to get food, you have to do these things. So it's hard.

I haven't worked since I got the oldest boy. I live off aid. You have a court order where the father pays the court. No matter how much he pays, you only goin' to get fifty dollars of it. He does that, but he's just not involved with the babies. He's a security guard.

You're takin' care of those babies from the time they come home from the hospital. You know, the mother's doin' nothin' for 'em. You're doin' everything for that baby. If I let her take that baby out of here and take him to a crack house, I'm responsible 'cause I know what's goin' on. So it was a lot of conflict. I couldn't let her take the baby. I had to watch him. This is somethin' I had to do. There's nothin' else you can do except let the baby go be put in a foster home, and I'm not about to let that happen. So I did it for the first. I didn't never expect to have another one, you know. With the first one they see that you mean business, that you goin' to do what you say you goin' to do. But that don't faze them, that don't faze them.

My mom's been real good. She's been real good about helping me with the first one and then the second one, but this time she's like "If you do that, you won't never come out of it. I don't think you should go ahead and keep on takin' her babies for her." Which I can understand in a way, you know, because I don't have the space for 'em. I'm lookin' for a place now. I really don't have the room for 'em. And these babies take up a lot of time, you know; they take up a lot of your time. The youngest one is in this program for slowly developed children. Her teacher comes now on Tuesdays and Thursdays, comes down and teaches her. You know, you go to the clinic every week, the special baby clinic, the neurology clinic. The first thing they say in the hospital is it has to do with cocaine because she was exposed to cocaine. And that's hard. And I hate that labelin' them children like that, but it's the truth.

A Hard Life

I don't feel so much angry. I feel as though even if she was to get herself straightened out, it would be hard for me to give them children up, you know, 'cause I feel as though they've been neglected, something's been taken away from them. The mother has been taken away from them. They don't know her, and if you just take these kids and give them back to her, that's goin' to be hard on the children. How are you goin' to explain? You know, the children don't understand what's goin' on. They know their grandmother right now is the mother, and it would be hard for 'em. They don't have no contact with her, don't see her. That's goin' to be hard on them, and I couldn't do that. I would rather raise them 'til they get of age, you know. Right now, there's nothin' much I can say to them. I can't say, "Well, this is your mother," 'cause I don't see her. She's supposed to come see 'em, and she never shows up. So I feel for the children more than I feel for the mother right now. I really do.

There's no sense gettin' upset. This is what you have to do. If you didn't see any sense in it, you wouldn't be doin' it. That's the way I look at it. These kids are special. They're special kids because they have been exposed to crack. So it's a lot of time, a lot of patience, and a lot of love. You've got to give it to 'em. So I enjoy it. I really do. I do it. I get tired sometimes. Sometimes I get frustrated, but I don't dwell on it, you know. I don't dwell on it. Right now the most important thing is these children. That's most important. Yeah, some people say that God is testing them and good things is goin' to come out of it.

Right now financially it's hard. I really need a place, I need a place of my own. Livin' in this apartment is not good for the kids. It's a problem all the time, problems with the neighbors, problems with the landlord. They come and use my phone when I'm not here. I have to keep it locked in my bedroom, and then I can't hear it. At the time I took this place, it was just me, and I was workin'. I thought once I earn some money, I'll get out of here. Once I got the grandbabies, all that stopped, you know. Life is hard, it's really hard. It's always somethin', always, always somethin'.

STRETCHING THE WELFARE CHECK

David Zucchino

David Zucchino is the author of *Myth of the Welfare Queen: A Pulitzer Prize–Winning Journalist's Portrait of Women on the Line.* The following excerpt from his book features Odessa, a poor black woman in Philadelphia who has custody of four of her grandchildren: Jim, Kevin, Delena, and Brian. By following Odessa's activities on the day that she picks up her welfare check, Zucchino shows how she manages to support her grandchildren on the small amount of money she receives. Odessa stretches her welfare check by taking advantage of store specials and shopping at flea markets and pawn shops. She also earns a few extra dollars by using her car as a taxi for her neighbors, and she supplements her family's diet by fishing in a local creek. Despite her cost-saving measures, Zucchino writes, Odessa still has to budget her money carefully to ensure it lasts the entire month.

I had come to take Odessa to the welfare office. It was check day. Under the numerical system set up by the Department of Public Welfare, Odessa was a Number Three. The numbers ranged from zero to ten, determined by the last digit of a recipient's welfare account number. Each digit assigned its owner to a certain day on which a welfare check was to be issued. Number Three happened to fall on this particular Wednesday, a late August day so hot and still that even by early morning a fine yellow haze had begun to suffocate Allegheny Avenue.

Odessa was sitting in the shade of her front porch, rocking gently in a rusted metal lawn chair. She was sipping hot coffee from a Dixie cup. She had bought it, as she did most mornings, for fifty cents from the Spanish man around the corner who sold fresh coffee from his porch. Buying the coffee was part of a daily routine that settled Odessa's nerves and added a certain tenuous structure to her life. In the afternoons she would pay another Spanish man a dollar for a *pincho* dripping with spicy grilled meat. And toward evening, when the hint of a breeze had begun to insinuate itself along the sidewalk, she would send one of the boys with a dollar to buy a bag of hot peanuts from Donald the Peanut Man. The rich aroma of charcoal and smol-

Excerpted from *Myth of the Welfare Queen: A Pulitzer Prize–Winning Journalist's Portrait of Women on the Line*, by David Zucchino (New York: Scribner, 1997). Copyright © 1997 by Simon and Schuster, Inc. Reprinted with permission.

dering peanut shells at dusk was Odessa's regular reminder that another day was dying. . . .

The Welfare Office

The financial exchange was located inside a squat green building smeared with white graffiti. It was a check-cashing business, one of many in the city that contracted with the state Department of Public Welfare to disburse bimonthly welfare payments. The bulk of the cash went to recipients of Aid to Families with Dependent Children, or AFDC, which is what citizens and politicians alike mean when they refer to "welfare." Odessa and her four grandchildren were among some 240,000 people in Philadelphia receiving AFDC cash. That meant at least 15 percent of the city's population was dependent every two weeks on a trip to a financial exchange center.

Inside the exchange, Odessa saw four lines of people waiting to be served by four women who sat behind thick Plexiglas shields, looking bored and vaguely put upon. The lines were long but orderly, and they moved quickly. Virtually everyone in line was black or Hispanic, for the exchange was in the heart of North Philadelphia. Most of the recipients were women trailed by sleepy-eyed children. They scolded their kids, took thumbs out of their mouths, wiped their snotty noses. The long, dark room was filled with the sounds of idle chatter. Many of the people in line knew one another, at least by sight, connected month after month by their shared Number Three. With the quiet conversation, the sudden squeals of children, the slow shuffle of feet moving forward, and the steady *snap, snap* of the clerks counting currency, the place had the look and sound of a bank.

Odessa selected the shortest line and, to pass the time, read the signs on the walls. One showed a drawing of Uncle Sam below the message *We Want to Cash Your Income Tax Check*. Another sign read, *Count All Money and Food Stamps Before Leaving Window*. Others read, *Children to Be Kept at Side or Outside*, and, *Today Is Number Three*. It seemed to Odessa that the welfare people spent too much time making signs and not enough time issuing checks. She hated waiting in line; it made her legs ache and her feet swell, especially on days as hot and miserable as this one.

As the line inched forward, Odessa saw a neighbor woman and waved at her. The woman smiled and waved back. Nobody minded being singled out in the welfare line, because so many people from the surrounding neighborhoods were on welfare. In the next line, in fact, was one of Odessa's nephews, who was waiting to pick up his food stamps. Odessa yelled his name. He looked back and grinned and shook his fist at her.

Odessa made a fist back at him. She loved to clown with all her relatives. The Boones were a roughhouse kind of family.

"Let's go at it right here!" she hollered, and she feigned a move toward her nephew. "Or would you rather go outside where all these people won't see you get a butt whipping from an old lady!"

Everyone in line was laughing now and watching the nephew, who raised both fists in a boxer's pose and yelled out, "Just let me get my stamps and I'll fight you for your check!"

"I'll whip you, and take your stamps, too!" Odessa said, but then she turned away and moved to take her place at the window, where the woman behind the glass was beckoning her forward.

Odessa produced her state welfare card with her color photo, which she hated because her hair looked flat and ragged, and because she was only half smiling. The clerk punched Odessa's welfare account number into the computer, which spit out a pink slip of paper containing Odessa's name and the cash amount due: $201.50. Odessa signed it. The woman counted out ten crisp $20 bills, a single dollar, and two quarters, and handed the whole amount to Odessa. She also passed her a tan coupon book stamped with a drawing of the Liberty Bell and the words *U.S. Department of Agriculture Food Coupons*. Inside was $84 worth of food stamps.

Odessa stuffed the coupon book into her purse. She folded the $20 bills and tucked them under her blouse and beneath her bra. The money had to last her the next two weeks, and thieves were everywhere.

The Stamp Men

She walked outside, where a stocky young man blocked her way.

"Stamps!" he yelled out. "Stamps! Seventy!"

Odessa pushed her way past the man, staring at him with contempt. The man shrugged and shouted "Stamps!" at the next woman who walked through the doorway. Just inside, a security guard was bent over the *Daily News*, ignoring the stamp man as he offered to pay cash for people's food stamps.

Odessa despised stamp men. They were neighborhood hustlers who bought food stamps for less than their face value. This particular stamp man was offering a good price—seventy cents on the dollar. Some offered just fifty cents. Odessa knew some welfare recipients who sold their stamps this way, usually to raise cash for drugs. Her drug-addicted daughter Brenda had done it before Odessa took over her AFDC payments and stamps. Odessa knew, too, that it wasn't only stamp men who bled the system. Plenty of merchants paid cash for stamps at discount, then turned them in for the face amount.

Even some drug dealers accepted food stamps, though at steep discounts. Over on North Hutchinson Street, a few blocks from Odessa's place, the Rivera gang accepted food stamps for green-cap crack, though at just twenty cents on the dollar. Some gangs offered to sell drugs on credit to welfare recipients; they required addicts to hand over their welfare ID cards until check day, when the dealers would accompany them to the financial exchange to recover their cash—plus interest.

The whole wicked business sickened Odessa. People like the stamp men only fed the notion that welfare recipients were cheats and drug addicts, when in fact most of the welfare people she knew played by the rules. She thought of welfare as part of God's bounty. To cheat the system would be to cheat the Lord.

The drug dealers were the worst offenders, she thought. Many of them had wives and girlfriends on AFDC, though Lord knows they didn't need the money. But there was no way for the welfare people to know that the women were supported by their drug-dealing men. Dealers did not exactly report their income. So as far as the welfare department knew, it was providing checks to needy women with dependent children. Odessa would feel her blood pressure rise when-ever she drove by the dealers' row houses and saw the elaborate new iron grillwork that had transformed their homes into fortresses against police raids. She would shake her head at the sight of a new BMW or Lexus parked out front.

"They ruin it for people who really need welfare—and there's plenty that do need it," Odessa said as she left the exchange center.

With the cries of the stamp man still ringing in her ears, Odessa walked to the deli next door. Inside she ordered the same treat that she allowed herself every time she picked up her cash. She sat down and ate the $1.75 special—a spicy hot sausage with relish, catsup, and onion, plus a cup of coffee with a free refill. It seemed extravagant, but she needed it to help steel herself for the next two weeks. There would be many days ahead when she did not have $1.75. So now she luxuriated in the sweet, hot spray that filled her mouth when she bit into the steaming sausage. As she ate, she told herself that she was actually saving money. The sausage so satiated her hunger that she decided she would forgo her usual lunchtime *pincho* and her dollar bag of roasted peanuts that afternoon.

Back home, Odessa climbed the steps and collapsed into the lawn chair on her porch. Her legs ached from the long wait in line. She was out of breath. The heat and humidity aggravated her asthma. She needed her nebulizer. She reached behind her and banged on the liv-ing room window and shouted to her grandson, "Jim! Bring me my machine!" Jim hauled the contraption out to the porch and plugged it in. Odessa took the mouthpiece from him and inhaled deeply. Soon the knot in her chest faded and she began to breathe normally. Now she could think about money.

The Budget

She tried to set up a budget for the next two weeks. The way she fig-ured it, with her AFDC check and stamps, and with $980 she had received on the first of the month for her grandson Brian's and her Supplemental Security Income (SSI) payments, she would have $216 left to pay for food and incidentals. Most of her income was already allotted for the phone bill, which was fattened by her grandson Darryl's collect calls from prison and her own calls back home to Georgia. She had to pay for gas for the Caprice, Pampers for the twins, sneakers for the boys, snacks for the kids every afternoon, and her past due gas bills from the previous winter.

Her biggest outlays were for the electric bill, which usually ran $280 a month, and for past due bills. She tried to cut back on electricity, but she needed at least two hours a day to prepare meals on her electric stove. And the kids needed hot water from the electric water heater for their baths. She had taken enough cold baths as a child; her grandchildren deserved better. She also ran her trash-picked air conditioner all day long in July and August. The device seemed to drink up electricity, but she needed it to help control her asthma, and Kevin's and Brian's too.

Odessa reached beneath her blouse and withdrew the welfare money from her bra. She counted out $60 for Integrity Meats on Front Street and tucked it beneath her left thigh. Integrity had the cheapest bulk meat in the neighborhood. For $60, she could buy a case of turkey wings, a case of turkey legs, twenty pounds of chicken wings, a package of oxtails, a box of chicken backs, and four packs of pork chops. Most of it she would store in her big upright trash-picked freezer.

She took another $20 bill and slipped it beneath her right thigh. That was for Murray's food store. Murray's was having a special—buy one pack of frozen meatballs, get one free. For $20 she could buy the meatballs, plus frozen beef patties and several boxes of mashed potato mix.

She counted out another $120 and dropped it on the chair between her legs. That was the amount she had spent the previous month at SAV-A-LOT, the big discount food center. The money would have to pay for another month's supply of nonperishables, such as canned goods, toilet paper, barbeque sauce, catsup, tuna, and dried beans.

More Expenses

There would be new expenses this month, with school starting the following week. The kids would need snack money for school—fifty cents a day each for Brian and Delena, a dollar each for Jim and Kevin. On the other hand, Odessa would save a small amount on breakfasts. The schools provided free breakfasts for low-income children, which included just about every child in the neighborhood. Even so, her kids sometimes ate breakfast at home *and* at school.

Odessa looked at the three little mounds of cash around her lap and wondered whether to promise the kids their regular monthly trip to Stacy's, the all-you-can-eat family restaurant in the Northeast. The kids loved driving up on a Sunday afternoon and gorging themselves on shrimp, pork chops, and fried fish at the all-you-can-eat buffet.

Sometimes they refilled their plates half a dozen times. But last month Odessa had miscalculated; she had thought the price was $1.99 per child. When the family arrived, she saw that it was $2.99. She did not want to disappoint the kids, so she paid the higher price. But now, thinking about it, she knew she would have to forgo Stacy's this month. Movies were out, too. She normally let the kids go see a movie once a month. Not this month. . . .

Odessa scooped up the three cash piles tucked around her lap. She folded the money into a little roll and tucked it back beneath her bra. She had allocated the entire $201.50, including the $1.75 she had spent on the hot sausage. She had picked up her welfare payment less than an hour ago, and already she felt broke.

Christmas

And then there was Christmas. It was only August, but Odessa's Christmas planning had already begun. Christmas was the highlight of the year for her and the grandchildren. She planned for it like a miser, tucking money away here and there, month after month, to pay for layaway gifts. In fact, the frozen turkey legs she planned to buy at Integrity Meats that week were for Christmas dinner. She would pack them in the freezer and resist until December the temptation to thaw them and cook them up.

She had begun paying for her grandchildren's first Christmas gift back in March. Ollie, her late sister's husband, had bought on layaway a Hooked on Phonics set containing audiotapes and books designed to improve reading ability. Ollie did not read well. He was determined to become literate. But that spring he was laid off from his job as a substitute custodian for the city school district. He couldn't make the Hooked on Phonics payments. They were $58 a month for four months, and he still owed for three months. Odessa offered to take over the payments. Her grandchildren were all good readers, but she wanted to give them an advantage the schools did not offer. And she wanted to improve her own stunted reading ability; just reading the electric bill was a struggle for her. By August, Odessa owed only one more payment. Soon Hooked on Phonics would be hers.

Once she got her hands on the set, she decided, she would hide it at her mother's place on Howard Street. One reason was to keep the grandchildren from finding it; they loved to root around in her closets. But the main reason was to keep it away from Brenda, who still dropped by the house whenever she needed food or a place to sleep. Two years earlier, Odessa had spent months paying for the grandchildren's Christmas toys and then hid them in her bedroom closet. Just before Christmas, Brenda stole every last gift and sold each one for cash to buy crack. She stole Odessa's trash-picked VCR and TV set, too.

Odessa vowed she would never again let Brenda ruin Christmas. Now she hid everything at her mother's house. Already that summer, she had bought two other Christmas gifts. That Saturday, she had driven up to the flea market on State Road and paid $50 from her SSI check for a used stereo for Jim. She had it tested by her son Fred, who pronounced it fit. That same day, she also had gone to a pawn shop and paid $7 for a used video game to give Brian for Christmas. The game cost $75 new, so Odessa was quite pleased with her savings.

She had many ways to cut corners and save money. She did not clip coupons, because few stores in North Philadelphia honored coupons. But she did drive to dollar stores and grocery stores and meat markets every few days, checking prices and asking about sale days. She was a regular at the Salvation Army donation centers, too. She would wait in the parking lot for people to pull up in cars to drop off donations. If she saw something she liked, she would ask for it. People almost always obliged her. Most of them, in fact, told her they admired her initiative. She got her favorite mop that way—one of those high-tech mops that allow you to wring out the sponge without bending over. It came with a brand-new replacement sponge, too. She also got an entire set of stainless steel cooking pots one day from a man dropping off donations.

Taxi Service

To earn extra cash, Odessa relied on the old Caprice. A car was a luxury for many people in North Philadelphia. Several of her neighbors relied on buses and subways, which were usually reliable but often required great outlays of time for the most basic errands. Odessa figured that most people would rather travel by car to pick up their welfare checks instead of taking public transportation. She began charging people a $5 round-trip fee to drive them to the financial exchange, wait outside at the curb, and drive them back home. She knew no one would complain about the price; she always felt flush and ready to spend money when she picked up her check. Everybody did. It was the highlight of most people's week. What was $5 at a time like that?

The same principle applied to grocery shopping. Many people took the bus to Cousin's supermarket on Allegheny Avenue, but they dreaded taking the bus back home while loaded down with bags of groceries. Odessa would stand at the store exit and offer rides to shoppers struggling with heavy bags. People on the street called this "haking." Like most hakers, Odessa charged between $5 and $10, depending on the distance. Most people were glad to pay. On most days she earned at least $50 for a few hours' work.

Odessa found ways to stretch her food budget. Sometimes her sister-in-law Lorraine gave Odessa cornmeal, flour, and rice that she had earned for helping distribute food to the needy in West Philadelphia. During hunting season, Odessa filled her freezer with squirrel, rabbit, and venison that her sons Willie and Israel shot on their hunting jaunts. She helped clean the meat herself. And all spring, summer, and fall—and just about anytime the temperature crept above fifty degrees—Odessa went fishing. She called herself a fishing fool. On certain summer mornings she would drive to Howard Street, pick up her mother, drive to West Philadelphia to dig worms at a vacant lot, then speed across the Ben Franklin Bridge to a secluded fishing spot hidden behind willow trees at a narrow bend in Woodbury Creek in southern New Jersey. On good days they would return home with fifty good-sized perch. Bertha Boone didn't eat fish, so Odessa would clean the whole load of perch and stuff them into her freezer. Most summers, she and her mother caught enough perch to last Odessa's family most of the next winter.

TRYING TO LEAVE THE INNER CITY

Janie Bryant

In the following selection, Janie Bryant tells the story of a single mother, Melissa Brown, who hopes to escape her bad neighborhood and find a larger home for her family. As Bryant explains, Brown has three children of her own, as well as legal custody of two children who were abandoned by their mother. Other family members and friends often live with Brown on a temporary basis, and her home is growing crowded. The author describes Brown's search for a better place, including the many obstacles she faces: Landlords in nicer neighborhoods will not accept her as a tenant because she has too many children and not enough money. Despite her determination to find a safer home for her family, Brown seems destined to remain in her deteriorating house in one of the worst sections of town. Bryant is a reporter for the *Virginian-Pilot*, a newspaper based in Norfolk, Virginia.

Another day is winding down. Parents call in children, suppers simmer on stoves, and families blend lives around kitchen tables and TV screens.

It's the same way at 216 Gleep St. in Portsmouth, Virginia. Yet it's different.

Night is falling, and Melissa Brown is hoping that her family will not deal with the darkness in Fairwood Homes much longer.

It is a bleak neighborhood even in the daylight.

Melissa's 14-year-old daughter dreams of a pretty house and a bedroom painted red. Melissa pictures a place big enough for her family of six to spread out, maybe give her 15-year-old son his own room.

Michael would like that, too. And he'd like to see grass for a change, not the muddy yard that blends into the pothole-filled court where they live.

They'd all like to get far away from the charred shell of a house nearby that sits like an open wound.

That's where Melissa's sister used to live. Where her 7-year-old niece died in a house fire in August 2000.

Her family isn't the only one trying to get out of Fairwood Homes, a sprawling World War II–era complex slowly making way for redevelopment.

Hundreds of residents know that one day they will get a notice telling them that they have no choice.

For a lot of them, that's how they got there to begin with.

A Night in Their Lives

At 5 P.M. on a winter night, Michael slides a copy of *The Sixth Sense* into the VCR.

It's scary, someone warns Pierre, the 7-year-old.

"I ain't no sissy no more," he says, squeezing closer to the television.

"At least I'm not the one scared to go under the house," he says, reminding his older brother of some recent feat of courage.

Melissa raises her eyebrows. This is news to her.

Bravery will not matter tonight, though.

The movie becomes just one more noise in a living room brimming with competing conversations, the siren-sounds of whining babies and the constant antics of siblings.

This week, Melissa's family has expanded to 10. There are two babies she's keeping for a friend who's having domestic problems. And Melissa's daughter's best friend is staying through June 2001 to finish out the school year. Her family has moved to North Carolina.

Then there's Melissa's mother, who is here so her daughter can devote more time to the search for a new home.

The living room they are crammed into is a stark contrast to the home with the imposing staircase that Bruce Willis is climbing in the movie that nobody is watching.

Sometimes neighborhoods Melissa can drive to seem just as far from her reach.

Hope and Despair

The dingy white units that dot the streets of Fairwood Homes might not be any worse than a lot of old dwellings in the poorest neighborhoods of any city.

There's just so many of them.

The sprawling decline has inspired city leaders to conclude that the only thing to do is start over. They plan to purchase the privately owned land in phases and replace the houses with an office park and possibly light industry or a shopping center.

For now, it's block after block of monotonous gloom. A neighborhood that inspires one question:

Why do people live here?

Stacey Bond, an officer in the neighborhood civic league, tried to tell City Council members one night.

Some residents are just poor, she said. Others have bad credit. For some, it's both.

She told them she didn't expect them to solve poverty. She just wanted them to understand.

"We're trying to put a face to the area, instead of everyone thinking that we are all crack-headed, welfare-receiving mothers with 10 children," she said.

"We want you to know that we're just poor. And poverty isn't a crime."

That's a common sentiment in Fairwood Homes.

It's as if they have to defend themselves against a stereotype that condemns them. As if city officials and maybe even other residents want to rid Portsmouth of more than deteriorated housing.

The feeling lays on them like a suffocating weight. One more thing that makes them feel hopeless.

Melissa Brown knows that feeling.

A blustery wind kicks up outside and the country curtains with the blue-trimmed ruffles fall down behind Melissa's head, exposing miniblinds that have scissored precariously.

Melissa and Michael wrestle with the blinds. She tells him to just take them down; she isn't planning on taking them to the new home, anyway.

She has an appointment to see a two-story home in Brighton in two days, and she is hopeful, talking as if it's certain.

Hope can be a powerful thing.

It's driven her to box up many of their possessions and put them in storage.

Only four family photos, including one of Kenetra, the niece killed in the fire, hang on the living room wall. The rest have come down, leaving nails poking out, exposing the chalky shade of lilac blue she'd hoped would brighten the room.

For months now, Melissa has acted like a new bride, setting aside certain household purchases—colorful print curtains from Wal-Mart and candles and pictures of angels she ordered from Home Interiors.

So Pierre is sent outside to throw away the blinds, and Michael is instructed to fold the curtains away.

Yes, hope can be a powerful thing. Sometimes it springs up even in places like Fairwood Homes.

Love and Laughter

Michael climbs on the couch to rig a heavy white bedspread, so it'll block the cold. The wind blows it up in the middle, making it look like a heart pulsing in the window.

Four-year-old Tiffany is trying to sit still on a Sam's Club–size box of baby wipes, eating saltines while Melissa braids her hair.

Now and then, Melissa's toddler, MJ, babbles, trying to break into conversations.

Melissa asks him to say "Elmo" and "Big Bird."

"Mam-Ma," he answers.

Michael heads to the kitchen and ladles some stew. He grabs a package of saltines and a small bottle of orange drink and heads for the sofa to try to get back into the movie.

The chatter and crying and confusion in the room is something like an orchestra during its tune-up.

"Michael, that TV is kind of loud," Melissa says as he turns up the volume.

"I know," he says. "Y'all talk too much."

Melissa turns her attention to helping Tiffany count on a Sesame Street toy, and the TV volume climbs.

"Michael, turn the volume down on the TV," she says in a voice that finally brings it down.

"That's why I stay in my room," she says, rubbing her head.

In reality, she is usually in the middle of her brood.

Even when she goes to her room to sleep, MJ and Tiffany share her bed. After Kenetra died, 12 people piled into Melissa's room, nieces and nephews who wanted to feel safe.

"I wasn't scared," Michael says.

"Whatever," Melissa answers.

She tells the children that the stew is cool now and instructs them to wash their hands. Michael's friend, Mario, brings Melissa a bowl.

"All of your food is good," says Mario, with a 12-year-old's impish charm.

He's followed his nose to Melissa's house many nights, and he joins the other children, sitting and standing around a round pedestal table in the kitchen.

The kitchen is a little more cheerful than the rest of the house. Melissa painted the walls and cabinet a lemon yellow. A matching cloth covers the table and bright-red curtains hang at the window.

Mario comes out of the kitchen after a short while, rubbing his stomach appreciatively.

I'm going to have to charge you restaurant fees, Melissa tells him.

He sits down and starts doing a dance, like a cha-cha, in his folding chair. Soon, he is up in the middle of the room and the other youngsters have joined him, trying out steps as Melissa laughs and calls out instructions.

"It's back-in-the-day stuff," Mario says, his way of saying old-fashioned.

The grim conditions fade away. Family fun takes center stage.

At one point, a gust of wind blows up and everyone pauses to listen.

It sounds as if it could lift that white spread on the window like a sail and knock over the house before a bulldozer does.

"I think we just need to get out of this house before it falls down," Melissa says.

She says it glibly, though her determination ebbs and flows, between confidence and self-doubt.

Melissa puts her monthly income at $1,100, a combination of baby-sitting proceeds, child support and public assistance.

She's paying $360 a month to live in Fairwood Homes. She figures she can afford a rent of $500. She's paid off an assortment of small debts, hoping that a landlord will give her a chance.

Already, she has searched newspaper ads and soaked up gas driving around Portsmouth neighborhoods such as Mount Hermon and Cavalier Manor. She spots "For Rent" signs, takes down numbers, makes phone calls.

It's about as much fun as beating the streets for a job without a high-school degree.

One landlord told her right off. The house, she said, wasn't big enough for Melissa's family.

Melissa has learned that on top of everything stacked against her— the money, the lack of education—she's got five other liabilities.

Her children.

Feeling Safe

Pierre darts through the living room for something, making everyone laugh as he stretches his T-shirt to hide his underwear. He's getting ready for a bath.

Tiffany comes out of the bedroom, dressed in warm, blue sleepers. I want a kiss, she says, stalling her bedtime.

She'll cry until her mother comes in, but first Melissa has to get MJ to sleep. Tiffany tries to rush the process.

Rock-a-my-baby. . . Rock-a-my Moma and MJ. Rock-a-my baby on a re-trop, she croons, fudging her way through the lullaby.

MJ's eyelids are droopy, but he's not giving up.

He will run off more steam, entertain his siblings, even have a bath first.

By 9:30, the living room has almost emptied.

Melissa is finally dropping off to sleep, with MJ and Tiffany curled up behind her. Pillows are pushed against the window to block the cracks that let in the wind.

Mario has been called home, and the older children are gearing down for bed, too.

Melissa's teen-age daughter, Michelle, and her friend, Shanda, have been sitting cross-legged on their beds, sharing secrets and listening to rap music. As it gets later, they start to burrow under blankets.

Melissa tells them that they have attitudes. She tries to shrug off this stage and prides herself on being a friend to her children, especially in their adolescent years.

She knows those years are hard.

Melissa was 13 when her mother had to give up her children because she got too sick to care for them. Melissa spent the next five years passed from an aunt's home to foster care.

At 34, her face still takes on the look of a sad teen-ager when she talks about it.

She had only one foster parent who gave her anything close to a mother's love.

That woman, dead now, taught Melissa everything she knows about cooking and shopping and managing money.

Taught her she needed to be able to take care of herself without a man.

Her real mother had already taught her about love.

As much as she loved that foster mother, Melissa remembers how she would lie face down on the sofa and cry to go home.

Reunited as adults, Melissa, her six siblings and their mother are close, almost clingy. It's as if they are trying to recover those lost years. They drew closer after Kenetra died, even vigilant.

Their lives are a mix of hard realities and happy moments. They move in the protective orbit of a proud family.

A world where children who don't expect family members to sock away money for college still can count on a birthday party where an infinite supply of aunts and uncles sacrifice to bring cash and gifts.

Her upbringing gave Melissa an affinity for the homeless. Made her more ready to open her already-crowded home. Taught her what children need.

No matter what, her children will feel safe. They will know that they are loved.

It is something she considers a gift, and she extends it beyond the boundaries of family.

Married at 18 and divorced nine years later, Melissa has three children of her own—Michael, Michelle and MJ. The other two, she took in as babies. Pierre first, then his sister, Tiffany.

For a long time, Melissa hoped their mother would get her life back together. Now, those children are family. She would fight to keep them.

This is not a world where parents slow down their careers to have 2.5 children. Or where charity means donating canned goods to a faceless stranger.

No one here can look the other way.

Michael heads for the bathroom, carrying a towel and a black box of toiletries.

At 15, he already has his mother's soft heart. He'll feed the stray dog or take care of the black cat that no one else wants.

A paper sign on his bedroom door reads "Michael's Pet Palace."

His iguana lives in one tank, a home the lizard is now sharing with a frog. A cage holds the cockatoo his uncle gave him.

And in a 50-gallon aquarium is Steeler, a small black fish with a gold stripe.

Relatively speaking, that fish has more living space than anyone else in the house.

The cockroaches are there, too, in Michael's room, and in the bathroom and in the kitchen at night, crawling up and down the washing machine.

Residents of Fairwood Homes complain that roaches and rodents are increasingly creeping into the crevices of their homes as the first stages of redevelopment disturb the earth.

Melissa's mother, Lona Sparrow, pulls out a notebook and starts going through mail she brought with her. It will be another two hours before she nods off on the living room sofa.

Her sock feet rest on the floor, twitching now and then.

She will be up and down all night. With practiced stealth, she will fix more bottles, change diapers and rock babies.

The rest of the house will sleep to the fountainlike gurgling of the aquarium, the whining wail of a neighborhood dog and the oceanlike sound of the wind.

That's a good night in Fairwood Homes. Residents complain of teen-agers who rove the area trying to scare them and drug dealers who peddle their poison, even in daylight.

The houses are described as matchboxes, so quick to ignite that more than one-third of the city's fire fatalities since 1980 have occurred there.

But on this night, the acrid smell of smoke does not herald another disaster.

Great Expectations

The two-story house in Brighton sits along a short, narrow lane off busy Elm Avenue, not far from the shipyard.

The front steps are pulled away from the porch a little, a sign that this house could be one more disappointment. But one step inside is heartening for Melissa.

The landlord has taken pride in this house.

A new, sand-colored carpet stretches throughout, and a creamy vinyl shines in the foyer and kitchen.

The house, probably built in the 1920s, has old-fashioned charm, and Melissa likes the French doors that lead to a front parlor. She stands in a wide hallway and muses about how her whole house could fit in this one area.

Michael has started to picture an upstairs room with a walk-in closet as his bedroom. His sister likes a room at the front.

It is a bright house with lots of windows. Red-tip shrubs peek over a sill.

The children stand outside with an aunt, while Melissa fills out the application in the kitchen. She finishes and stands near the landlord as he scans it.

She looks like a young girl squirming under a teacher's gaze.

She points out that she put down three children. She has legal custody of two others, she explains. But she didn't list them because the mother could get herself together and want them back at any time.

Technically, that's true.

It is a sad paradox for a woman worn down by rejection.

She is suddenly apologizing to a stranger for what she's proudest of and the things in life she loves most.

By the next day, Melissa doesn't seem excited about the house in Brighton.

She did not lie awake thinking about how nice it would be to have a kitchen big enough for the whole family to eat together. Or how those green counters would set off the colors of her new curtains.

Hope seems to be slipping away.

She bats around other ideas. She says she's called to see if she might be eligible for a U.S. Department of Urban Development home.

Maybe she could wait awhile, fix this place up, paint the walls again. But it wouldn't add the space they need or replace the decaying wood that would accelerate a fire.

Still, she will not rush to get the papers proving her monthly income to the Brighton landlord.

A week later, he will stop by to see what's become of her. She still won't have all of the papers, and he says he'll come back.

But he doesn't. He doesn't call, either. She stops trying to reach him, too.

She thinks maybe that house wasn't the right one after all.

A New Day

Another day is dawning. Parents herd children from sleepy beds to school buses.

It's the same way at 216 Gleep St.

Melissa's mother rises once again and changes yet another diaper. Then the baby in the playpen starts to whimper.

She picks him up and calls out, "Michael! Pierre! Michelle!"

Pierre emerges from his room, taking sleepy steps. He grabs the faded jeans and plaid shirt he pulled out the night before, then goes to the kitchen and opens the refrigerator door, as if hoping the coolness will wake him.

Michelle comes out next, grabbing a wash cloth out of the curtained hall closet.

Tiffany turns on the television, but doesn't end up watching.

Melissa gets up and starts calling the stragglers. She sits in the living room, in the middle of everything, orchestrating the motion of her children.

Before long, the front door opens and her sister's five children troop in, bundled like Eskimos and toting an assortment of knapsacks.

A few minutes later, the door opens again and her neighbor's two children come in to wait for the bus so their mother can go on to work.

Seventeen people are in the house now, and all of the electronic toys seem to be playing over the morning news. The children are on the sofa, perched like baby birds.

Tiffany heads off for her preschool bus at 7:30. Ten minutes later, Shanda, Michelle and Michael leave to catch their bus. Pierre and the neighbor's two are next.

Already it seems quieter, and everyone takes a moment to listen to something Diane Sawyer is saying on ABC's *Good Morning, America*.

Then the last of the schoolchildren leave with their uncle, who has come to give them a ride.

Here I go again, says 7-year-old Keone. He's got to go to computer lab, then physical education, he says, ticking off his school day.

Melissa looks amused. Life should be so hard.

ORGANIZATIONS TO CONTACT

The editors have compiled the following list of organizations concerned with the issues presented in this book. The descriptions are derived from materials provided by the organizations. All have publications or information available for interested readers. The list was compiled on the date of publication of the present volume; the information provided here may change. Be aware that many organizations take several weeks or longer to respond to inquiries, so allow as much time as possible.

American Enterprise Institute for Public Policy (AEI)
1150 Seventeenth St. NW, Washington, DC 20036
(202) 862-5800 • fax: (202) 862-7177
website: www.aei.org

AEI sponsors research on a wide range of national and international issues, including economics, government regulation, health care, and taxes. Among its publications are the monthly magazine *American Enterprise*, which has advocated reform of America's public welfare system, and the reports "How Poor Are the Poor?" and "Welfare Reform: Four Years Later."

The Brookings Institution
1775 Massachusetts Ave. NW, Washington, DC 20036-2188
(202) 797-6000 • fax: (202) 797-6004
e-mail: brookinfo@brook.edu • website: www.brookings.edu

The institution is devoted to nonpartisan research, education, and publication in economics, government, foreign policy, and the social sciences. Its principal purposes are to aid in the development of sound public policies and to promote public understanding of issues of national importance. It publishes the quarterly journal the *Brookings Review*, which periodically includes articles on poverty, and numerous books, including *The Urban Underclass*.

Cato Institute
1000 Massachusetts Ave. NW, Washington, DC 20001-5403
(202) 842-0200 • fax: (202) 842-3490
e-mail: cato@cato.org • website: www.cato.org

The institute is a libertarian public policy research organization that advocates limited government. It has published a variety of literature concerning poverty in its quarterly *Cato Journal* and in its *Policy Analysis* series.

Center of Concern
1225 Otis St. NE, Washington, DC 20017
(202) 635-2757 • fax: (202) 832-9494
e-mail: coc@coc.org • website: www.coc.org

Center of Concern engages in social analysis, theological reflection, policy advocacy, and public education on issues of justice and peace. Its programs and writings include subjects such as international development, women's roles, economic alternatives, and a theology based on justice for all peoples. It publishes the bimonthly newsletter *Center Focus* as well as numerous papers and books, including *Opting for the Poor: A Challenge for North Americans*.

Center on Budget and Policy Priorities
820 First St. NE, Suite 510, Washington, DC 20002
(202) 408-1080 • fax: (202) 408-1056
e-mail: center@center.cbpp.org • website: www.cbpp.org

The center promotes better public understanding of the impact of federal and state governmental spending policies and programs primarily affecting low- and moderate-income Americans. It acts as a research center and information clearinghouse for the media, national and local organizations, and individuals. The center publishes numerous fact sheets, articles, and reports, including *The Safety Net Delivers: The Effects of Government Benefit Programs in Reducing Poverty*.

Coalition on Human Needs
1120 Connecticut Ave. NW, Suite 910, Washington, DC 20036
(202) 223-2532 • fax: (202) 223-2538
e-mail: chn@chn.org • website: www.chn.org

The coalition is a federal advocacy organization that works in such areas as federal budget and tax policy, housing, education, health care, and public assistance. It lobbies for adequate federal funding for welfare, Medicaid, and other social services. Its publications include *How the Poor Would Remedy Poverty* and the *Human Needs Report*, a biweekly legislative newsletter.

Economic Policy Institute
1660 L St. NW, Suite 1200, Washington, DC 20036
(202) 775-8810 • fax: (202) 775-0819 • (800) 374-4844 (publications)
e-mail: epi@epinet.org • website: www.epinet.org

The institute was established in 1986 to pursue research and public education to help define a new economic strategy for the United States. Its goal is to identify policies that can provide prosperous, fair, and balanced economic growth. It publishes numerous policy studies, briefing papers, and books, including the titles *State of Working America* and *Declining American Incomes and Living Standards*.

The Heritage Foundation
214 Massachusetts Ave. NE, Washington, DC 20002-4999
(202) 546-4400 • fax: (202) 546-8328
e-mail: info@heritage.org • website: www.heritage.org

The foundation is a public policy research institute dedicated to the principles of free competitive enterprise, limited government, individual liberty, and a strong national defense. The foundation publishes the monthly newsletter *Insider* and *Heritage Today*, a newsletter published six times per year, as well as various reports and journals.

National Alliance to End Homelessness
1518 K St. NW, Suite 206, Washington, DC 20005
(202) 638-1526 • fax: (202) 638-4664
e-mail: naeh@naeh.org • website: www.naeh.org

The alliance is a national organization committed to the ideal that no American should have to be homeless. It works to secure more effective national and local policies to aid the homeless. Its publications include *The Ten Year Plan to End Homelessness*, *Turning the Financial Corner from Survival to Prosperity*, and the weekly *Alliance Online News*.

National Center for Neighborhood Enterprise (NCNE)

1424 Sixteenth St. NW, Washington, DC 20036
(202) 518-6500 • fax: (202) 588-0314
e-mail: Info@ncne.com • website: www.ncne.com

The center promotes self-sufficiency among residents of low-income communities and works for the revitalization of urban neighborhoods. NCNE publishes the periodic newsletter *In the News* and the briefs "What's Wrong with the Debate About Faith-Based Initiatives" and "Bridging the Gap: Strategies to Promote Self-Sufficiency Among Low-Income Americans."

National Council of La Raza (NCLR)

1111 Nineteenth St. NW, Suite 1000, Washington, DC 20036
(202) 785-1670 • fax: (202) 785-0851
website: www.nclr.org

NCLR is a national organization that promotes civil rights and economic opportunities for Hispanics. It provides technical assistance to Hispanic organizations engaged in community development, including economic development, housing, employment and training, business assistance, health, and other fields. The council publishes a quarterly newsletter, *Agenda*, as well as other issue-specific newsletters on poverty.

National Student Campaign Against Hunger and Homelessness (NSCAHH)

233 N. Pleasant Ave., Amherst, MA 01002
(800) 664-8647 • (413) 253-6417 • fax: (413) 256-6435
e-mail: nscah@aol.com • website: www.pirg.org/nscahh

NSCAHH is a network of college and high school students, educators, and community leaders who work to fight hunger and homelessness in the United States and around the world. Its mission is to create a generation of student/community activists who will explore and understand the root causes of poverty and who will initiate positive change through service and action. It publishes the quarterly newsletter *Students Making a Difference* as well as numerous manuals, fact sheets, and handbooks.

Population Reference Bureau (PRB)

1875 Connecticut Ave. NW, Suite 520, Washington, DC 20009-5728
(800) 877-9881 • (202) 483-1100 • fax: (202) 328-3937
e mail: popref@prb org • website: www.prb.org

PRB gathers, interprets, and disseminates information on national and world population trends. Its publications include the quarterly *Population Bulletin* and the monthly *Population Today*.

Poverty and Race Research Action Council (PRRAC)

3000 Connecticut Ave. NW, Suite 200, Washington, DC 20008
(202) 387-9887 • fax: (202) 387-0764
e-mail: info@prrac.org • website: www.prrac.org

PRRAC was established by a coalition of civil rights, antipoverty, and legal services groups. It works to develop antiracism and antipoverty strategies and provides funding for research projects that support advocacy work. It publishes the bimonthly newsletter *Poverty and Race*.

Progressive Policy Institute (PPI)
600 Pennsylvania Ave. SE, Suite 400, Washington, DC 20003
(202) 547-0001• fax: (202) 544-5014
website: www.ppionline.org

PPI develops policy alternatives to the conventional liberal-conservative politi-cal debate. It advocates social policies that move beyond merely maintaining the poor to liberating them from poverty and dependency. Its publications include *Microenterprise: Human Reconstruction in America's Inner Cities* and *Social Service Vouchers: Bringing Choice and Competition to Social Services.*

BIBLIOGRAPHY

Books

Rebecca M. Blank   *It Takes a Nation: A New Agenda for Fighting Poverty.* Princeton, NJ: Princeton University Press, 1997.

Robert Desjarlais   *Shelter Blues: Sanity and Selfhood Among the Homeless.* Philadelphia: University of Pennsylvania Press, 1997.

Peter Edelman   *Searching for America's Heart: RFK and the Renewal of Hope.* Boston: Houghton Mifflin, 2001.

Barbara Ehrenreich   *Nickel and Dimed: On (Not) Getting By in America.* New York: Metropolitan, 2001.

William M. Epstein   *Welfare in America: How Social Science Fails the Poor.* Madison: University of Wisconsin Press, 1997.

Ronald F. Ferguson and William T. Dickens, eds.   *Urban Problems and Community Development.* Washington, DC: Brookings Institution Press, 1999.

Mary Ellen Hombs   *American Homelessness.* Santa Barbara, CA: ABC-CLIO, 2001.

Paul A. Jargowsky   *Poverty and Place: Ghettos, Barrios, and the American City.* New York: Russell Sage Foundation, 1997.

LeAlan Jones and Lloyd Newman with David Isay   *Our America: Life and Death on the South Side of Chicago.* New York: Scribner, 1997.

Robin D.G. Kelley   *Yo' Mama's Disfunktional! Fighting the Culture Wars in Urban America.* Boston: Beacon Press, 1997.

Gary MacDougal   *Make a Difference: How One Man Helped Solve America's Poverty Problem.* New York: Truman Talley Books, 2000.

Susan E. Mayer   *What Money Can't Buy: Family Income and Children's Life Chances.* Cambridge, MA: Harvard University Press, 1997.

Katherine S. Newman   *No Shame in My Game: The Working Poor in the Inner City.* New York: Alfred A. Knopf and the Russell Sage Foundation, 1999.

Benjamin I. Page and James R. Simmons   *What Government Can Do: Dealing with Poverty and Inequality.* Chicago: University of Chicago Press, 2000.

Harrell R. Rodgers Jr.   *American Poverty in a New Era of Reform.* Armonk, NY: M.E. Sharpe, 2000.

David Simon and Edward Burns   *The Corner: A Year in the Life of an Inner-City Neighborhood.* New York: Broadway Books, 1997.

William Julius Wilson   *When Work Disappears: The World of the New Urban Poor.* New York: Alfred A. Knopf, 1996.

Periodicals

Mary Jo Bane   "Poverty, Welfare, and the Role of Churches," *America*,
                            December 4, 1999.

Bruce Bartlett   "The Ominous Income Gap," *World & I*, September
                            1997. Available from 3600 New York Ave. NE,
                            Washington, DC 20002.

Pam Belluck   "Razing the Slums to Rescue the Residents," *New York
                            Times*, September 6, 1998.

Laurent Belsie   "Who's Up from Poverty, and for How Long?"
                            Christian Science Monitor, October 1, 2001.

Steven A. Camarota   "Importing Poverty: Immigration's Impact on the Size
                            and Growth of the Poor Population in the United
                            States," September 1999. Available at www.cis.org.

Stephanie Coontz   "When the Marriage Penalty Is Marriage," *New York
and Donna Franklin   Times*, October 28, 1997.

Samuel Francis   "Immigration into Poverty," *Conservative Chronicle*,
                            September 6, 2000. Available from PO Box 11297, Des
                            Moines, IA 50340-1297.

Annette Fuentes with   "Poverty in a Gilded Age," *In These Times*, June 12,
Frances Fox Piven   2000.

Peter C. Goldmark Jr.   "Reclaiming America's Inner Cities," *Christian Science
                            Monitor*, July 22, 1997.

Kay Humowitz   "At Last, a Program That Works," *City Journal*, Winter
                            1997. Available from the Manhattan Institute, 52
                            Vanderbilt Ave., New York, NY 10017.

Albert R. Hunt   "Faith-Based Efforts: The Promise and Limitations,"
                            Wall Street Journal, August 12, 1999.

Jesse Jackson   "Leave No American Behind," *Liberal Opinion Week*,
                            July 27, 1998. Available from PO Box 880, Vinton, IA
                            52349-0880.

Andrew Jacobs   "Even as Economy Booms, Working Poor Often Just
                            Scrape By," *New York Times*, November 30, 1997.

Marianne M. Jennings   "My Neighborhood Ruined, Thanks to HUD," *Wall
                            Street Journal*, June 19, 1997.

Nancy L. Johnson   "Should Congress Fight Poverty by Promoting
and Patricia Ireland   Marriage?" *Insight on the News*, December 13, 1999.
                            Available from PO Box 91022, Washington, DC
                            20090-1022.

David Cay Johnston   "Can Americans Give More, and Not Hurt?" *New York
                            Times*, April 4, 1999.

Peter T. Kilborn   "Memphis Blacks Find Cycle of Poverty Difficult to
                            Break," *New York Times*, October 5, 1999.

Jonathan G.S. Koppell   "When Private Hands Do the Public's Work," *Los Angeles Times*, December 19, 1997. Available from Reprints, Times Mirror Square, Los Angeles, CA 90053.

Kathryn Larin   "Should We Be Worried About the Widening Gap Between Rich and Poor?" *Insight on the News*, February 9, 1998.

Michael Lind   "The Case for a Living Wage," *New Leader*, September 2001.

Don Matthews   "The Free Market: Lifting All Boats," *Freeman*, April 1997. Available from Foundation for Economic Education, 30 S. Broadway, Irvington-on-Hudson, NY 10533.

Ellen Mutari   "Self-Sufficiency: An Elusive Goal," *Dollars and Sense*, July 2001.

James L. Payne   "Why the War on Poverty Failed," *Freeman*, January 1999.

Wendell Primus   "What Next for Welfare Reform?" *Brookings Review*, Summer 2001.

William Raspberry   "Three-Point Recipe for Alleviating Black Poverty," *Liberal Opinion Week*, August 31, 1998.

Robert Rector, Kirk A. Johnson, and Patrick F. Fagan   "Understanding Differences in Black and White Child Poverty Rates," *A Report of the Heritage Center for Data Analysis*, May 23, 2001. Available from 214 Massachusetts Ave. NE, Washington, DC 20002-4999.

James Ridgeway   "Ministering to the Poor: Church and State, Together Again," *Dollars and Sense*, March 2001.

Joe Sexton   "In a Pocket of Brooklyn Sewn by Welfare, an Unraveling," *New York Times*, March 10, 1997.

Mark Skousen   "How Many of You Are on Food Stamps?" *Ideas on Liberty*, December 2000. Available from Foundation for Economic Education, 30 S. Broadway, Irvington-on-Hudson, NY 10533.

Betsy Taylor   "Poverty, Race, and Consumerism," *Poverty and Race*, July/August 1997. Available from 3000 Connecticut Ave. NW, Suite 200, Washington, DC 20008.

Chris Tilly   "Next Steps for the Living-Wage Movement," *Dollars and Sense*, September 2001.

D. Mark Wilson   "Increasing the Mandated Minimum Wage: Who Pays the Price?" *Heritage Foundation Backgrounder*, March 5, 1998. Available from 214 Massachusetts Ave. NE, Washington, DC 20002-4999.

Robert Wilson   "Slash-and-Burn Urban Renewal," *New York Times*, July 9, 1999.

INDEX

affirmative action
  impact on inner-city blacks, 51
Affirmative Discrimination (Glazer), 66
Aid to Families with Dependent
    Children (AFDC)
  benefits, and out-of-wedlock births,
    49
  ending of, 94, 102
  see also welfare
Alinsky, Saul, 131
Ambrose, Christopher, 26
American Demographics (journal), 15
American Housing Survey, 39
Anderson, Elijah, 53, 142
Asian Americans
  child poverty rates for, 83
  poverty among, 82
Association of Community
    Organizations for Reform Now
    (ACORN), 87–88

Baker, David, 132
Bane, Mary Jo, 49
Bassi, Lauri Jo, 49
behavioral theories
  on causes of poverty, 47–51
  fails to recognize powerlessness
    as issue, 64–65
Bell, Ralph, 9
Besharov, Doug, 23
Betrayal of the Urban Poor, The
    (Slessarev), 63
births
  of "crack babies," 23–24
  to native-born vs. immigrant
    women, 83–84
  out-of-wedlock
    among children of broken
      homes, 70
    is not correlated to welfare
      benefits, 49
    link with poverty, 71–72
    welfare dependency and, 42, 65
    workfare and, 111
  to welfare recipients, 19
blacks
  buying power of, 15–16
  child poverty rates for, 83
  decline in marriage among, 53
  immigration as economic threat to,
    84
  inner city, impacts of civil rights
    laws on, 51–52
  men, homicides among, 22–23

obesity among, 42
  poverty rate among, 82–83
  structural theory of poverty among,
    53–54
  vs. whites, poverty among, 14–16
  duration of, 59
Blank, Rebecca M., 20, 57, 99
Bond, Kit, 129
BRIDGE Housing Corporation (San
    Francisco), 131, 132
Brocht, Chauna, 33, 34
Brown, Melissa, 156–64
Bryant, Janie, 156
Bush, George W., 115, 121, 123

Cabrini-Green project (Chicago), 9,
    22
Caldwell, Oralann, 110
Carlson-Thies, Stanley, 96
Carter, Jimmy, 131
Census Bureau, U.S. *See* U.S. Census
    Bureau
children
  of broken homes, out-of-wedlock
    births among, 70
  education of, and family structure,
    75
  families with, income by structure,
    72, 73
  poverty rates, by race and ethnicity,
    83
civil rights laws
  impacts on economic
    opportunities, 51
Clinton, Bill, 94, 129
Collins, Patricia Hill, 18
Commerce Department, U.S. *See* U.S.
    Department of Commerce
Community Builders, The, 131
community-development
    corporations
  housing built by, 128–31
Community Service Society, 32
Community Solutions Act, 117–18
Concerned Citizens of South Central
    Los Angeles, 131
Confronting Poverty (Heclo), 18
Consumer Expenditure Survey (U.S.
    Department of Labor), 37–38
Conte, Andrea, 113, 114
Corcoran, Mary, 69
Cordero-Guzman, Hector, 30
"crack babies," 23–24, 145–46
crack cocaine, 23–24

Crenshaw, Kimberle Williams, 19
crime
    in housing projects, 10
    is limited to small numbers of the
        poor, 24–25
    in poor neighborhoods, 20–24
    reasons for fear of, 22
    victimization rates for, 21
Cuomo, Andrew, 86

Daily People (newspaper), 91
Danziger, Sheldon, 49, 77
Day, Sara, 98, 99, 100
De Leon, Daniel, 91
Denton, Nancy, 63
Diallo, Amadou, 27
divorce
    link with welfare receipt, 49
    poverty and, link between, 69–70
    problems caused by, 70–71
Dollar General stores
    job-training program of, 112–14
Dreier, Peter, 87
drug use, 23–24
Duff, Christina, 98
Duffy, Marcia Passos, 32
Duncan, Greg J., 53

economic opportunities
    impacts of civil rights laws on, 51
    importance of, in ending poverty,
        62, 67
Economic Policy Institute, 32, 34
Edelman, Marian Wright, 17
education
    as barrier for young immigrants, 30
    of children, and family structure, 75
    link with employment
        inner-city children do not learn,
            11–12
elderly
    poverty among, 45
    duration of, 59
Ellwood, David T., 49
employment market
    changes in, impact on inner-city
        blacks, 51, 66–67
End of Equality, The (Kaus), 52
Enterprise Foundation, 130

Fagan, Jeffrey, 53
Fagan, Patrick F., 68
faith-based initiatives
    government support of, can help
        reduce poverty, 115–20
    con, 121–23
    obstacles to, 122–23
families
    budget breakdown for, 34

changes in, as cause of poverty,
    60–61
with children, income by structure,
    72, 73
poverty among, 33–34
single-parent, are more likely to be
    poor, 68–78
welfare as destructive of, 42–43, 49
fertility rates
    among Mexican vs. non-Hispanic
        blacks, 84
Foner, Nancy, 29
Fordice, Kirk, 129
Francik, Jeffrey M.A., 9
Fromstein, Mitchell, 110
Fuller, Millard, 131

Garfinkel, Irwin, 49
Gasson, Thomas I., 91
Gilder, George, 65
Glazer, Nathan, 65
Goldsmith, Steve, 119
Goode, Wilson, 118
Gore, Al, 121, 123
government, federal
    retreat from housing programs by,
        129
    support of faith-based initiatives by,
        can help reduce poverty, 115–20
    con, 121–23
guns
    related violence and, in urban
        ghettos, 22

Habitat for Humanity, 131, 133
Hall, Tony, 118
Harwood, Richard, 14
Heclo, Hugh, 18
Hispanics
    child poverty rates for, 83
    fertility rates for, 83
    poverty among, 80, 82
Hoffman, Saul D., 53
Holzer, Harry J., 53
homicides
    among black men, 22–23
Hood, Glenda, 119
households
    classified as poor, conditions of,
        37–38
housing
    cost of, 86
    low-income, role of nonprofits and
        community-development
        corporations in building, 128–35
    rules for, 132
    space, among poor vs. overall
        population, 38–39
    see also public housing

Howard, Delmarco, 119
Howd, Aimee, 92
Hubbard, Antoinette, 99, 100
hunger
  in U.S. is limited, 40–41
Husock, Howard, 124

immigrants
  young, struggles of, 25–31
immigration
  is responsible for rising poverty
    rate, 79–84
  of unaccompanied minors, 26
income
  annual, and poverty level, 32
  basic needs and, gap between,
    33–35
  effects of education and work ethic,
    75–76
  household, effects of divorce on,
    69–70
  median, 33
    of families with children, by
      structure, 72
  minimum wage, and cost of
    housing, 87
  personal, 37
  why family structure affects, 74–75
Industrial Areas Foundation, 131
inner cities
  attempt to leave, 156–64
  change of role in neighbors in,
    137–41
  guns and related violence in, 22
  lack of job opportunities in, 63–67
  loss of working/middle class from,
    11–12
  responsibilities of a grandmother
    in, 142–47
  struggles of young immigrants in,
    25–31
Institute for Wisconsin's Future, 99
It Takes a Nation: A New Agenda for
  Fighting Poverty (Blank), 20, 57

Jackson, Jesse, 14
Janis-Aparicio, Madeline, 90
Jarret, R.L., 53
Jencks, Christopher, 53
jobs
  in inner cities, 10–11
  inner-city, impact of employment
    market changes on, 51
job-training programs
  corporate involvement in, 112–15
Johnson, J.H., 53
Johnson, Lyndon B., 37, 89, 94
Journal of Blacks in Higher Education,
  The (journal), 15

Karp, Nathan, 89
Kasarda, John D., 10, 53
Kaufman, Risa E., 17
Kaus, Mickey, 52
Kharfen, Michael, 92
Kimm, Sue, 42
King, Martin Luther, Jr., 64
Kowtz, Roger, 108
Kukla, Genevieve, 93

Labor Department, U.S. See U.S.
  Department of Labor
Lazio, Rick, 125, 129
Leo XIII (pope), 91
Levitan, Mark, 33, 34
living standards
  for poor people has improved,
    35–43
  poverty-level income and, 32
living wage
  is necessary to help working poor,
    86–88
  con, 89–91
Local Attachments: The Making of an
  American Neighborhood, 1850–1920
  (von Hoffman), 128
Local Initiatives Support Corporation
  (LISC), 130
Losing Ground (Murray), 49

MacDonald, Heather, 101
Magallan, Joel, 28
Magnet, Myron, 47, 48, 49
Maguire, Kathleen, 21
marriage
  decline in, among blacks, 53
Massey, Douglas, 63
Matsuhashi, Yuko, 73
Mayer, S., 53
McElrath, Lisa, 101–102
McElrath, Rhafel, 101–102
McLanahan, Sara S., 49
Mead, Lawrence M., 50, 52, 65, 67, 96
Medina, Lucia, 137, 138–41
Medora, Malik, 105
middle class
  loss of, in inner cities, 11–12
Mincy, Ronald B., 53
minimum wage
  cost of housing and, 87
Morrice, Polly, 121
Moseley-Braun, Carol, 129
Murray, Charles, 49, 52, 65, 66, 129
Myth of the Welfare Queen: A Pulitzer
  Prize–Winning Journalist's Portrait of
  Women on the Line (Zucchino), 148

National Health and Nutrition
  Examination Survey, 40

National Income and Product
Accounts (U.S. Department of
Commerce), 37
National Low Income Housing
Coalition, 87
Neighborhood Reinvestment
Corporation, 130
*New American Blues: A Journey Through
Poverty to Democracy* (Shorris), 137
New Politics of Poverty, The (Mead), 65
New York City Housing Partnership,
131
Nifong, Christina, 112

obesity
poverty and, 41–42
Oliver, M.C., 53
O'Neil, June, 76

Panel Study of Income Dynamics, 75
Pastore, Ann L., 21
Payne, James L., 50, 52
Peirce, Neal, 86
Perales, Nina, 18
Personal Responsibility and Work
Opportunity Act (1996), 94, 101
new rules under, 102–103
Pollin, Robert, 90
Poole, Michael, 96
poor
crime is committed by small
numbers of, 24–25
numbers of, 9
Census Bureau overstates, 35–43
working, living wage is necessary to
help, 86–88
con, 89–91
population
changes in, by race and ethnicity,
82
poverty
belief and, in effort, 77
black
structural theory of, 53–54
vs. white, 14–16
causes for end of, 61
Census Bureau report overstates,
35–43
concentration of, in inner cities, 63
definition of, 35
differential reactions to, 55–56
divorce and, 69–70
duration of, 58–59
economic reasons for, 60
government support of faith-based
initiatives can help reduce,
115–20
con, 121–23
household conditions and, 37–38

housing space and, 38–39
hunger and, 40–41
links with crime are overstated,
20–24
long-term
economic factors behind, 57–62
the underclass and, 48–49
low-wage earners are trapped in,
32–34
among nontraditionally poor
families, 33
by race and ethnicity, 81
rates
for Asian Americans, 82
for blacks, 82–83
for college-educated, 33
for Hispanics, 80, 82
risk among single parents, 72–73
social problems and, 43
theories on causes of
bias about, and types of
solutions, 46
cultural/behavioral, 47–51
cultural inferiority, 18
structural/economic, 51–55
welfare acts to sustain, 52–53
Poverty in the United States, 1997 (U.S.
Census Bureau), 79
poverty level
income threshold for, 32, 81
Primus, Wendell, 95
Pruit-Igoe project (St. Louis), 9–10
public housing, 9
crime in, 10
plans to demolish worst of, 124
practical alternatives to, 124–27,
128–35
public opinion
on rising crime as problem, 21
on welfare policy, 96
Pyatok, Michael, 132

Race Matters (West), 54
racism
role in black poverty, 52, 54
Rector, Robert, 35, 97, 99
Reimers, David, 29
*Repairing the Ladder: Toward a New
Housing Policy Paradigm* (Husock),
124
Riis, Jacob, 39
Roberts, Dorothy E., 18
Robert Taylor project (Chicago), 9
Rockefeller, David, 131
Rodgers, Harrell R., Jr., 45
Roncek, Dennis, 9
Rouse, James, 130

Safire, William, 122

Seligman, Martin, 77
Sengupta, Somini, 25
Shaw, Clay, 97
Shorris, Earl, 137
Slessarev, Helene, 63
Sneed, Donna, 113–14
Spade-Aguilar, Maggie, 33
Sparrow, Lorna, 162
standard of living. *See* living standards
Steele, Shelby, 64
stereotypes
    negative impacts of, 19
    of the poor, 45
    of "welfare queen," 17–19
Sternlieb, George, 125
Street, John, 118
suburbs
    black population in, 16
    movement of working/middle class
        to, 11–12
surveys
    on rising crime as problem, 21

Talbert, Dennis, 120
Taylor, Julia, 93
Temporary Assistance to Needy
    Families (TANF), 94
Tenement Landlord, The (Sternlieb),
    125
Thom, Linda, 79
Thompson, Tommy, 96, 106, 109
Truly Disadvantaged, The (Wilson), 11,
    51
Tucker, Cassandra, 92
Turner, Cal, Jr., 113

U.S. Census Bureau
    estimates on the number of poor
        by, 9
    are overstated, 35–43
    among blacks vs. whites, 14
    fails to account for immigration in
        poverty numbers, 79–80
U.S. Department of Commerce, 37
U.S. Department of Housing and
    Urban Development, 124
    need of new role for, 126–27
U.S. Department of Labor, 37–38

von Hoffman, Alexander, 128

Wallerstein, Nina, 64
Wall Street Journal (newspaper), 98
War on Poverty, 89
    dependency as effect of, 42

Washington, Betty, 142
Washington, Reggie, 104
Washington Post (newspaper), 15
Watson, Kirk, 88
Watts, J.C., 117–18
Weinberg, Daniel, 80
welfare
    acts to sustain poverty, 52–53
    benefits, budgeting under, 100,
        148–55
    decline in, and work requirements,
        95
    as harmful to the poor, 50, 65
    impacts on hours worked, 76–77
    reform of
        has had mixed success, 98–100
        new rules under, 102–103
        in New York City, 103–104
        see also Personal Responsibility
            and Work Opportunity Act
            (1996)
    time limits on, 108
"welfare queen"
    as racial stereotype, 17–19
West, Cornel, 52, 54–55
whites
    vs. blacks, poverty among, 14–16
    duration of, 59
Williams, Omar, 105
Wilson, William Julius, 11, 51, 53–54
Wisconsin Works program, 96–97,
    106–107
    in rural vs. urban areas, 108–11
women
    black
        in labor force, 15
        "welfare queen" stereotype of,
            17–19
        fertility rates for, 84
        native-born vs. immigrant, births
            to, 83–84
Work and Gain Economic Self-
    Sufficiency program (Florida), 96
Work Experience Program (New York
    City), 104, 109
workfare
    out-of-wedlock births and, 111
    successes and failures of, 101–11
    in Wisconsin, 107
working class
    loss of, in inner cities, 11–12

Youngblood, Johnny Ray, 133

Zucchino, David, 148